A Kid's Guide TO New York City

GULLIVER TRAVELS

A Kid's Guide To

New York City

Gulliver Books
Harcourt Brace Jovanovich, Publishers
San Diego   New York   London

Written by Peter Lerangis
Illustrations and maps by Richard E. Brown
Designed by G.B.D. Smith

Printed in the United States of America
First edition
A B C D E

C·O·N·T·E·N·T·S

How to Use This Book

So, you're about to visit New York City! You'll be looking up a lot at all the tall buildings. And you'll be looking around, too, at all the people and colorful sights. But if you want to know about the best things to see and do, just look down from time to time—at this book!

You can read this book before you go, but don't forget to carry it with you while you're on your trip. Just like New York City, this travel guide is full of surprises—just for kids. There are pictures to color and maps to show you how to get around in New York City. You'll also find games to play and puzzles to do—perfect for long rides in planes, taxis, and subways. With this book you'll never have to worry about getting bored while the grown-ups are deciding what to do next.

T·R·A·V·E·L D·I·A·R·Y

My name is_____.

I live at_____,

in_____,_____.

My phone number is (_____) _____-_____.

I'm taking a trip to New York City. I'm traveling with_____

_____, and we plan to be away from home for

_____days.

My parents' full names are_____

and _____. In case of

emergency, they can be reached at _____,

where we are staying while on vacation. Or you can call

_____at (_____) _____-_____.

❖ ❖ ❖

(my picture)

Birthday_____

Age_____

Sex_____

Height_____

Weight_____

Eye color_____

Hair color_____

The first part of the book will tell you what it's like in New York City—the city's size, its weather, and its people. After that, there's a section full of interesting facts about the city's history.

Next, you'll find out how to get there—you can go by train, airplane, bus, or automobile. Just about every form of transportation goes to New York.

The biggest section of the book tells you what you can see in the city—the zoos, the skyscrapers, the boat rides, the beaches, and much more.

Trace your route to New York City

Whether by car, train, bus, or airplane, there was a route you had to follow to reach your destination. Color in the state where you live and draw a line tracing your path from home to New York City.

Once you know exactly what month you'll be in New York City, check the calendar on pages 118–119 to find out about some of the special annual events for kids.

For particular information about a place you want to visit, like the time it opens, the address, or the phone number, look in the appendix. Following the appendix, you'll find games to play in the car and the answers to the puzzles in the text.

At the very end of the book is an index which will tell you the page numbers for places and things you'll want to read about.

New York City is always changing. We've done our best to give you the latest information here, but it may change next week. You should always check with a phone call to make sure the place you want to go is open. There's a lot to see—so let's get started!

Will I Like New York City?

New York City is full of fun things to see and do—you can see jungle animals, go to the top of a 110-story building, and swim at one of the world's biggest beaches, all in the same day. Not only that, you'll be able to zoom to all of these places underground—on the world's largest subway system!

Interested? There's a lot more. Here are some other things you can find in New York City:

Did you know?

New York City is not only the nation's leading port, but the center for finance, publishing, fashion, and the arts.

- a theater group with only kids as actors
- a planetarium that projects the stars and the planets all around you
- a museum that's inside an aircraft carrier
- horse-and-buggy rides in the middle of the city
- a park with waterfalls, lakes, bridle paths, a children's zoo, a marionette theater, and even a castle on a hill
- the world's largest movie screen
- dinosaur skeletons as big as a house
- an old-fashioned seaport village with cobblestone streets

Maybe the only thing you won't like about your trip to New York City is that you won't get a chance to do everything. So plan on coming back again and again!

Did you know?
Seventeen million people visit New York City each year.

T·R·A·V·E·L D·I·A·R·Y

I want to see a lot of things while I'm in New York City. Some of the places that I've heard about are _____.

_____

I want to see these places because _____.

_____

❖ ❖ ❖

What's the City Like?

New York City is like nothing you've ever seen. Even if you're from another big city, you'll still be amazed by the size of New York.

First of all, New York has more people than any other city in the United States—over 7 million altogether! That's more people than in the states of Alaska, Idaho, Montana, Nevada, New Hampshire, North Dakota, Rhode Island, South Dakota, Vermont, and Wyoming put together! In fact, it's more people than live in some countries.

THE 5 BOROUGHS

The main part of New York City is called **Manhattan**—that's where most of the skyscrapers are and most of the people. It's hard to imagine, but Manhattan is actually an island about 15 miles long and 2 miles wide. To the west is the Hudson River, to the north the Harlem River, to the east the East River, and to the south the Upper New York Bay, which runs into the Atlantic Ocean. But Manhattan is only one part of New York City. Over the rivers and across the bay, there are 4 other sections, called *boroughs*. They are Brooklyn, Queens, Staten Island, and the Bronx.

Even though **Brooklyn**, south of Manhattan, is only part of New York City, it has more people than every other entire city in the U.S.—except Los Angeles, Chicago, and (what else?) New York City. In Brooklyn, people of many different nationalities settled, forming their own neighborhoods.

Did you know?

Manhattan is an Indian name, Brooklyn and Staten Island are from Dutch names, Queens is named after the Queen of England, and the Bronx is named after a Danish family.

The Bronx is north of Manhattan. Here you'll find a large zoo and Yankee Stadium. The Bronx got its funny name many years ago when it was rural land owned by a family whose last name was Bronck. When people went to visit them, they'd say, "We're going to the Broncks'." The name stuck, but the spelling changed.

Queens is just above Brooklyn. Kennedy and LaGuardia Airports are here, as are Shea Stadium, several exhibits left from the 1964–65 World's Fair, and more ethnic neighborhoods.

```
J   I   B   G   X   O   F   R   O   I   L   M   T   C   S
Y   A   V   R   K   Q   X   N   E   A   Y   X   H   B   A
P   F   R   Z   O   C   H   U   D   S   O   N   E   Q   N
Q   Y   B   O   R   O   U   G   H   T   Q   P   B   U   T
S   E   K   O   D   A   K   D   B   A   Y   Z   R   Y   B
Q   U   E   E   N   S   U   L   C   T   F   P   O   V   D
T   W   E   R   B   E   D   L   Y   E   N   E   N   E   S
P   M   A   N   H   A   T   T   A   N   K   O   X   R   H
U   F   S   K   G   U   E   D   G   I   R   P   F   R   C
Z   A   T   L   A   N   T   I   C   S   M   L   J   A   O
G   B   R   O   N   C   K   S   H   L   S   E   W   Z   Z
J   T   I   N   V   L   A   G   Z   A   R   D   M   A   M
Z   I   V   O   H   G   M   X   I   N   Q   K   R   N   V
H   T   E   W   S   I   W   J   L   D   M   U   P   O   H
W   O   R   L   D   S   F   A   I   R   J   K   V   L   U
```

Answer the questions below to discover what words you must find in the puzzle.

1. The smallest county in the United States is _____ .
2. The borough that has more people than all but 3 cities in the whole country is _____
_____ .
3. Brooklyn is a section of New York City known as a _____ .
4. Yankee Stadium is in _____ .
5. _____ is connected to Brooklyn by the longest suspension bridge in the world.
6. Kennedy and LaGuardia Airports are located in _____ .
7. The _____ River is to the west of Manhattan.
8. To the east of Manhattan is the _____ .
9. The Upper New York Bay runs into the _____ Ocean.
10. There are many animals in the Bronx _____ .
11. New York has more _____ than any other city in the United States.
12. The Bronx was named after a family known as the _____ .
13. The 1964–65 _____ was held in the borough of Queens.
14. South of Manhattan is the Upper New York _____ .
15. The world's longest suspension bridge is called the _____ -Narrows Bridge.

(Answers on page 129)

```
```

Staten Island is below Manhattan. Not all of it looks like a city—there are forests, lakes, and small houses in some areas. Staten Island connects with Brooklyn by way of the longest suspension bridge in the world—the Verrazano-Narrows Bridge.

Chances are that when people speak of New York City, they are talking about Manhattan. Most of the places mentioned in this book are in Manhattan, but there are plenty of things to do in the other boroughs, too! One thing to remember is that New York City is sometimes called just plain *New York*.

ALL THOSE PEOPLE!

Why are there so many people in New York City? Part of the reason is because it's one of the main seaports on the East Coast. Many immigrants from Europe must go through New York City before going on to other states. Another reason is that there are many businesses here, and that means a lot of jobs.

But one of the biggest reasons people live in New York City is because there's so much to see and do. Between the theaters, music, museums, stores, and sporting events, there seems to be something for everyone.

Between 7:00 and 9:00 in the morning and between 5:00 and 7:00 in the evening, you'll see huge crowds of New Yorkers rushing around. These are the rush hours—the times when everyone is going to or from work. Thousands of these people don't even live in New York City. They commute from many miles away—from places like Long Island, Westchester County, and New Jersey.

Did you know?

In Manhattan, there are more telephones than in Chicago, Queens, and Washington, D.C., put together.

GETTING AROUND
■■■■■■■■■■■■■■■■■■■■

Maybe the most important thing to bring on your trip to New York is a comfortable pair of shoes. That's because you'll be doing a lot of walking. Not very many people drive in New York City, except taxi drivers and truck drivers. Fortunately, New York is an easy city to get around in. Taxis are plentiful and the public transportation system is cheap and easy to use.

Did you know?

There are 6,400 miles of streets in New York City.

You'll be taking subways, buses, and taxis—and walking, of course. The sidewalks are always filled with people. In fact, don't be surprised if you find yourself on the same sidewalk as a famous TV, movie, or sports star—in New York, *everybody* walks!

Did you know?

The hottest months in New York City are July and August, with average temperatures in the low 80's. The coldest month is January, when the temperature sinks to the 30's and below.

THE WEATHER

The weather changes a lot in New York City. If you're traveling in the wintertime, bring a heavy coat, sweaters, and boots, because it can be windy, snowy, and freezing cold. In the summer, you'll need shorts because it gets hot and muggy. The best times to visit are in the spring and fall, when the temperatures are the most comfortable.

SAFETY TIPS
■ ■ ■ ■ ■ ■ ■ ■ ■ ■ ■ ■

When you're in New York City, you'll be looking around all the time—and so will the grown-ups you're with. But don't forget to keep an eye on each other at all times. You'll be in a strange city, and it's very crowded. Make sure to stay close together on busy sidewalks and in stores.

You'll be surprised at the way New Yorkers cross streets. They hardly ever pay attention to red lights. People don't get tickets for jaywalking here, but that doesn't mean you shouldn't be careful! *Always* look both ways when crossing—some of the drivers go awfully fast, even when there are a lot of people around.

Did you know?

New York City police are specially trained to help lost kids find their parents—and so are store owners who have a "Safe Haven" decal on their stores.

Did you know?

There are 12,000 yellow taxis on the streets of New York.

15

People on the streets are so close sometimes that it's easy for a pickpocket to snatch your wallet, watch, or even purse. It's always a good idea to keep whatever you're carrying close to your body, under your arm, and in front of you.

What happens if you get separated from the grown-ups? The most important rule is this: don't panic. People will help you. If there's a police officer nearby, go up and tell him or her what happened. If you don't see one, find an open area and wait a couple of minutes. Don't forget, the grown-ups are looking for you, and they're going to come back to the place where you were separated. If there are stores nearby, go into one and tell the shopkeeper what happened. Don't worry. You'll find your parents eventually.

New York City wasn't always the crowded and busy city it is today. You'll be surprised to learn how it began—and you can find out in the next section.

What do these traffic signs and signals mean?

1. Yellow

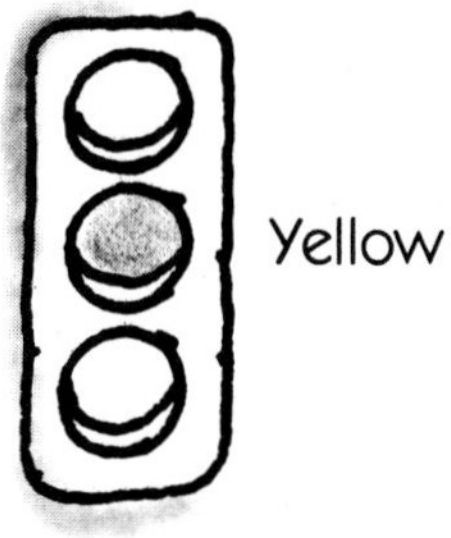

2.

3.

4.

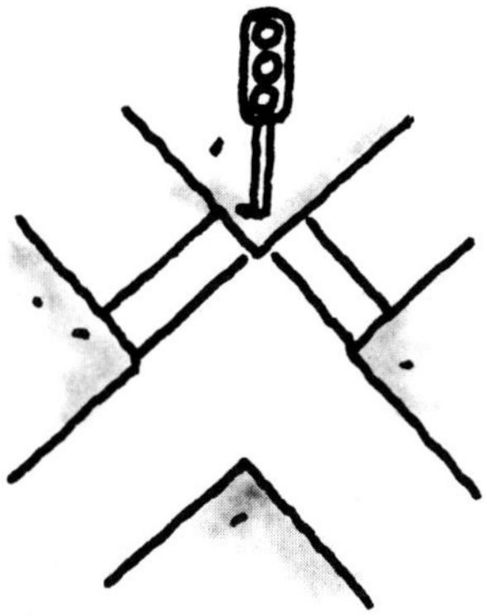

5.

1. _____   4. _____

2. _____   5. _____

3. _____

(Answers on page 129)

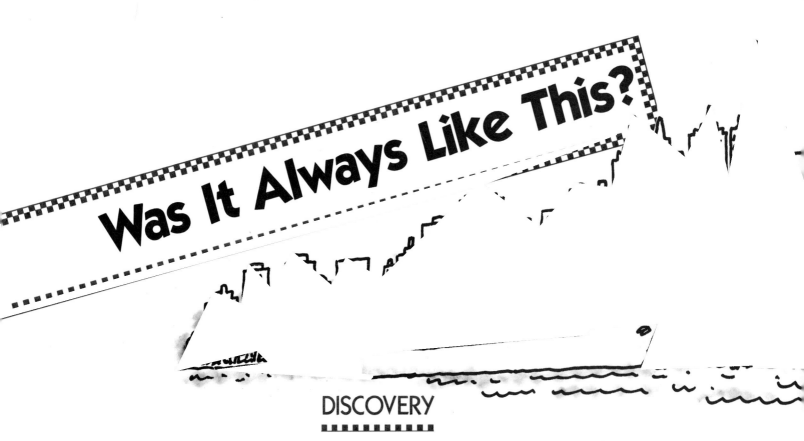

Was It Always Like This?

DISCOVERY

When you look at New York City today, most of what you see is man-made. Above ground, buildings are crowded side by side. The ground itself is covered with cement and blacktop. And underground are miles of power lines, cables, and subway tunnels.

But in 1524, when the native Americans who lived here caught sight of the first European explorer, New York City was a much different place. Manhattan had no buildings, no roads, no bridges—just endless forests, fields, streams, rolling hills, and small Indian villages.

That's what New York was like over 450 years ago when the explorer Giovanni da Verrazano sailed into Upper New York Bay. Like the other explorers of his

Did you know?

New York's first European settlers called the natives they met here the *Manhattan tribe*.

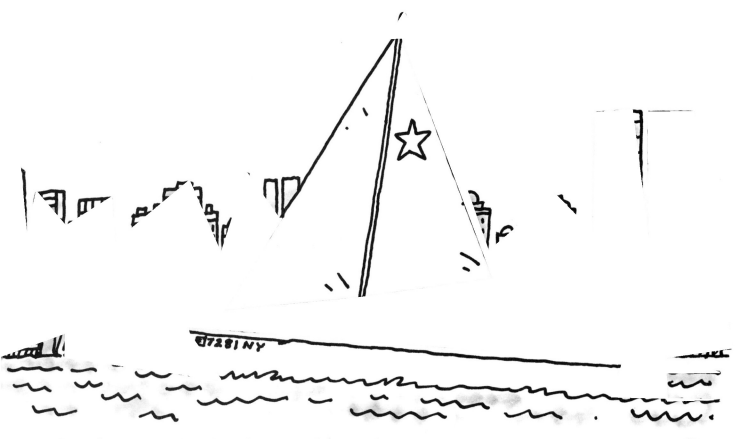

time, he was trying to solve a problem—he was looking for a faster and easier trade route from Europe to the Orient by sailing west, instead of traveling overland to the east. But what Verrazano found was the forests of what we now call New York City.

In 1609 the English explorer Henry Hudson went all the way up a river (the one now called the *Hudson River*) as far as the area around Albany. He, too, turned back, thinking he was a failure for not finding the Orient.

What these two brave explorers did find was a land new to the Europeans. That is why it became known as the *New World*.

Did you know?

Verrazano was an Italian explorer hired by the French. Henry Hudson was an English explorer hired by the Dutch.

FIRST EUROPEAN SETTLERS

The Dutch were the first to settle this new land. In 1624, only 4 years after the Pilgrims landed on Plymouth Rock, 110 people from Holland became the first New Yorkers—except that's not what they called

KNOW YOUR HISTORY

1. What the European explorers called the tribe of native Americans they met when they landed here.
2. The people of New Amsterdam built this at the northern edge of town to keep invaders away.
3. First New York explorer's nationality.
4. New York was named after him.
5. New York was covered with these when the explorers arrived.
6. The nationality of New York's first European settlers.
7. New Amsterdam was named after the capital of this country.
8. Peter Minuit bought Manhattan with these.
9. Explorers were trying to find a trade route to here by sailing west from Europe.

(Answers on page 129)

themselves. In fact, when a group of families decided to move to what's now Manhattan, they called it *New Amsterdam*, after Amsterdam, the capital of Holland.

BUYING MANHATTAN

The Dutch liked New Amsterdam so much that they decided to try to buy the whole island from the natives. One Dutchman, Peter Minuit, went to the forest on the northern tip of Manhattan to meet with a group of natives. He laid out a pile of trinkets. "I'll trade you these for all of this island," he said. The natives agreed, and the deal was made. How much were the trinkets worth? About $24—one of the cheapest bargains in history!

In the mid-1600s, New Amsterdam grew into a town of 1,500 people. A wooden wall was built at the very northern edge of the town to keep away invaders. Nowadays, instead of the wall there's a street—Wall Street!

Did you know?

When the first Dutch settlers arrived in New York, they chased away French settlers who had gotten there only hours before them!

■ ■ ■

The Indians who sold Manhattan to Peter Minuit were imposters—they didn't live in Manhattan at all. No wonder they sold it for a pile of trinkets!

■ ■ ■

Less than 20 years after New York was first settled, there were already 1,500 people there, speaking 18 different languages.

■ ■ ■

For about 1 year, in 1673, New York's name was changed to New Orange.

In 1664, the British took over and renamed the town *New York* after the Duke of York. New York grew and grew, right on through the Revolutionary War, when it became part of the United States.

NOT JUST ANOTHER CITY

But New York was just another city in the United States for many years, not the biggest and not the smallest. All that changed in 1825, when the Erie Canal was dug across New York State. Now ships could enter New York Harbor and go right through to the Midwest.

Almost overnight, New York became the most important city in the country. Year after year, more and more people came and thousands of buildings were put up. And the growth still hasn't stopped, even though the Erie Canal isn't as important as it used to be.

Did you know?

After the Revolutionary War, George Washington said farewell to his troops in Manhattan at Fraunces Tavern, which still stands today.

HERE COME THE IMMIGRANTS

In the early 1900s, boatloads of people from around the world (mainly Europe) entered the United States at New York Harbor. They came here for the same reasons people today still leave their homelands to live in the U.S.—to escape wars or poverty, to find religious or political freedom, or to follow a dream of new jobs, opportunities, and hope.

Their wide eyes must have been filled with fear and wonder as they sailed past the Statue of Liberty and landed on Ellis Island. There, their papers and their health were checked before they could go across the bay to Manhattan.

Arriving in their new world, many immigrants settled in neighborhoods with other people from their homelands. Their similar speech and customs helped

Did you know?

One out of every 2 people in the United States today either came to this country through Ellis Island or is descended from someone who did.

to make their move a little easier. Even today, as you walk through New York City, you can see the many different immigrant neighborhoods—Italian, Greek, German, Chinese, and many others—and hear the different languages spoken on the street.

THE SKYSCRAPER

Since Manhattan is an island, there wasn't much room for the city to spread out. The invention of the elevator helped solve that problem—buildings could grow upward! Before long, Manhattan could brag about the "world's tallest building." The year was 1899, and the building was 12 stories high. (It still stands today, at 15 Park Row.)

Over the next 35 years, thousands of buildings went up in Manhattan. It seemed that every few years a new "world's tallest building" was built. In 1913, the tallest one was the Woolworth Building (at Broadway and Park Place), paid for by the man who established Woolworth stores. It was so much taller than any

T·R·A·V·E·L D·I·A·R·Y

I _____ riding in elevators. The tallest building I've ever been in is the _____. It is _____ stories tall. I could see _____ from the top. The tallest building in my home town is _____. It is _____ stories high.

❖ ❖ ❖

other building that when it was lit up on the night it opened, people could see it from Long Island and New Jersey.

The Woolworth Building was not the tallest for long. Eighteen years later, the Chrysler Building went up— and then 4 years after that, the Empire State Building. It was hard for people to adjust to a 102-story building.

Today New York has not one, but two 110-story buildings—side by side. Together these make up the World Trade Center, in lower Manhattan.

Did you know?

In 1945, an army bomber crashed right into the Empire State Building in the fog! Fourteen people were killed and $1 million of damage was done.

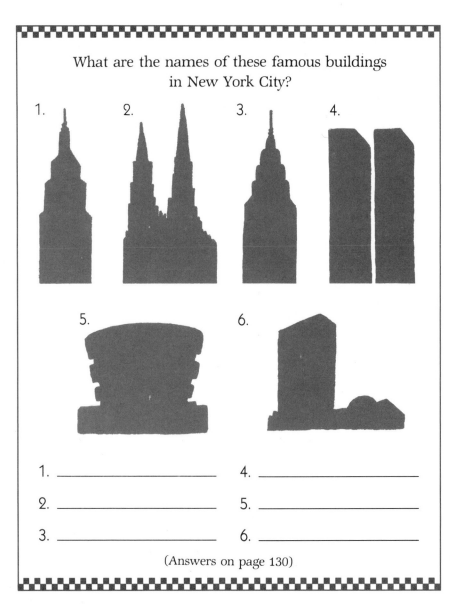

What are the names of these famous buildings in New York City?

1.
2.
3.
4.
5.
6.

1. _____   4. _____

2. _____   5. _____

3. _____   6. _____

(Answers on page 130)

Did you know?

One-quarter of Manhattan's land was added on, using dirt that was shoveled out when subways, tunnels, and building foundations were dug.

■ ■ ■

The earth that was dug up to make the World Trade Center was dumped right next door— it's the land that Battery Park City was built on top of.

WHY MANHATTAN DOESN'T SINK

Since Manhattan is an island with huge skyscrapers built right next to each other, you may wonder why it doesn't sink into the sea. It's because Manhattan is mostly an island of granite, a superhard, superstrong rock so thick that it hardly even feels the weight of the tall buildings. In fact, the entire 102-story Empire State Building weighs less than the granite and dirt that was dug up to build it. If you walk through Central Park, you can see big boulders of the dark gray granite peeking through the ground.

Today, New York City is still growing. Smaller buildings are being torn down and skyscrapers are being squeezed into narrow spaces. Not much is left from the days native Americans lived here. But one thing that does remain is a long, diagonal dirt path that went from one end of Manhattan to the other. It has been paved over many times and is still here today—it's called Broadway!

Now that we know a little bit about the history of New York City, let's begin our trip.

Did you know?

Nowadays there are builders who want to tear down skyscrapers to make even bigger ones on the same land.

That's where Great Great, Great Grandpops TEE-PEE was!

How Do You Get There?

YOU CAN FLY

The best part about flying to New York City is just before you land. That's when the airplane flies over Manhattan. All of a sudden the buildings seem to reach up out of the ground like steel mountains. And in between the buildings, the streets look like little canyons.

Did you know?

Since Shea Stadium is right near LaGuardia Airport, sometimes baseball players stop playing in the middle of a game when noisy planes take off or land.

T·R·A·V·E·L D·I·A·R·Y

We will be leaving from _____ and arriving

at _____ on _____ .

We will travel through _____ to

get to New York. New York City is _____ hours/ _____

days/ _____ miles from my home. Once we get to New

York, we will stay at _____ .

❖ ❖ ❖

You'll think there's no place to land. But don't worry—all three of New York's airports are outside of Manhattan. One of them, Newark Airport, isn't even in New York State—it's in New Jersey, but only about 20 miles from the city. The other two are in Queens. Kennedy Airport is the largest of them all, and has many international flights. LaGuardia is the one closest to Manhattan. There are buses, taxis, and limousines that go into Manhattan from each of the airports.

YOU CAN TAKE THE TRAIN

If you take a train to New York City, you may be in for a treat. Chances are you'll end up in the famous Grand Central Terminal. (Some people call it *Grand Central Station*, but that's really the name of the post office next door!) Be sure to walk through the main lobby—and look up. This is one of the highest ceilings you'll ever see. And also one of the strangest and most beautiful. There is a map of the constellations on it, with many of the stars marked by twinkling lights.

To see all the activity from above, just climb the wide marble stairs at the west end of the station. But you can get an even better view: At the top of the stairs turn left, go through an entrance marked Traffic Club of New York, and take the elevator to the fourth floor. There you'll find a glass hallway that looks out over the whole area.

Did you know?

There are 133 separate train tracks that go in and out of Grand Central Terminal.

■ ■ ■

On top of Grand Central Terminal, there's a 59-story building—and on top of *that*, there used to be a helicopter port.

There's something else pretty amazing in Grand Central Terminal—the "whispering wall." First go to the lower level. Then follow the signs to the Oyster Bar. Right before you get to the Oyster Bar, you'll pass through an open room that has white-tiled arches. The arches come to the floor in four places. Ask someone to stand up against one of those places and face the wall. Then you stand just opposite, where the other end of the arch comes to the floor. Face the wall and whisper something—tell the other person to whisper back. You'll hear the other voice as if he or she is standing right next to you!

If you arrive in New York City by train but don't go into Grand Central Terminal, you will be in Pennsylvania Station, which is all underground. If you come by bus, you'll get off at the Port Authority Bus Terminal. Since this is New York and there are so many people, all of these places are very large.

BRIDGES

Because Manhattan is an island, you have to go over or under a river to get there. There are many ways to do it—20 bridges and 22 tunnels, to be exact.

Some of the bridges are really worth seeing. At the southern end of Manhattan, there are 3 bridges in a row. They are the Brooklyn Bridge, the Manhattan Bridge, and the Williamsburg Bridge. The Brooklyn Bridge is the oldest (over one hundred years!) and most beautiful. It has long, crisscrossing cables. You can even walk across it on a pedestrian walkway. This will give you a spectacular view of the Manhattan skyline.

Did you know?

It's hard to believe, but when the Brooklyn Bridge was built in 1883, its towers were the tallest things in New York City.

Did you know?

It was hard to build a bridge in 1883. The creator of the Brooklyn Bridge was killed in an accident while it was being built. Then his son took over, and he was paralyzed for life in another accident.

■ ■ ■

At certain times of the day, you'll see a golden glow from two of the skyscrapers, the New York Life Building and the Metropolitan Life Building. That's because their domes are covered in 24-carat gold!

T·R·A·V·E·L D·I·A·R·Y

I _____ to go on bridges. I have been over _____ of them. My favorite bridge in New York is the _____ . We took it from _____ to _____ . We went through the _____ Tunnel. It connects _____ with _____ .

❖ ❖ ❖

Did you know?

The Triborough Bridge connects 3 boroughs—Manhattan, the Bronx, and Queens.

■ ■ ■

On July 4, the world's largest flag is flown from the Verrazano-Narrows Bridge.

At night, the Williamsburg and Manhattan bridges look like they have brightly lit caterpillars crawling across them. Those are the subway trains, which have tracks of their own alongside the roads.

The longest bridge in the city is the George Washington Bridge, in the northwestern part of Manhattan. Because its pillars are made of thick steel beams, the bridge might look unfinished to you. And you're right. The builders had planned to put cement around the pillars. But they thought the steel beams looked so beautiful when light showed through that they decided to leave them as they were.

Did you know?

Two billion people ride the New York City subways each year.

SUBWAYS

The New York City subway system is one of the modern wonders of the world—in fact, it is the largest rapid transit system anywhere. People may tell you it's dangerous and filthy, but it's not that bad. After all, 5 million people a week use it—and that's just during the morning rush hour! It's the quickest and cheapest way to get around in New York City, and probably the most fun.

The subway is like a long carnival ride. While the city is bustling above in the sunlight, the subway snakes along in dark, empty tunnels underneath. Take a look at a subway map (you can get a free copy at most stations) and you'll be amazed—each of those colored lines is a subway route. The tracks stretch for hundreds of miles. They go to practically every area of New York City—business districts, parks, beaches, baseball stadiums. They go underground, over bridges, under rivers, and through fields.

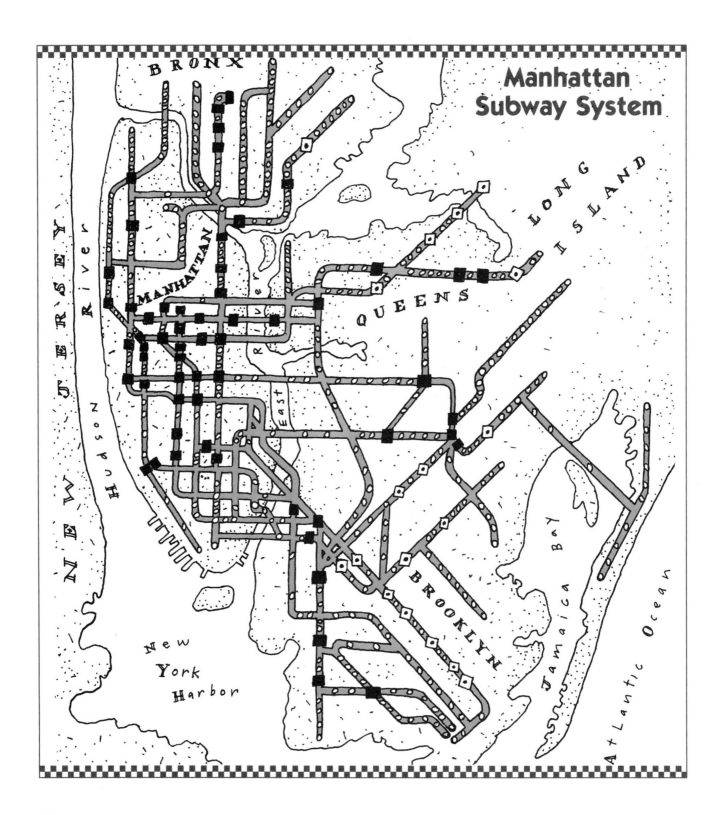

Manhattan Subway System

Many of the tunnels and stations date back to the early part of this century. Some of the stations have beautiful, old mosaic tiles on the walls. A lot of the subway stations have become grimy over the years, but these tiles show that they were once elegant places. If you're lucky, you'll hear a musician playing in the station while you're waiting.

Want to see something exciting? Ride in the very last or first subway car and look out the end window when the train is moving. But only do this if the car is pretty crowded and it's not late at night.

Did you know?

The first subway in New York City was built in 1904.

■ ■ ■

There are 240 miles of subway tracks under New York City.

T·R·A·V·E·L D·I·A·R·Y

The best subway station I've seen is _____,

because _____. I rode the

_____ subway to _____

to see _____. When we went on the

subway, I _____.

The people on the subway were _____.

I think subways are _____ ❖ ❖ ❖

Most of the time, the subway is perfectly safe—but you should pay attention to a few basic rules, just in case. It's not a good idea to show money, expensive jewelry, or gold chains. And if you are carrying a pocketbook, try to keep your hand on it when it gets crowded. If you have a wallet, put it in your front pocket. And always stay away from the edge of the platform. If you have to take the subway late at night, wait for it wherever there are the most people or within view of the token booth, and always ride in one of the middle cars of the train. Remember, a subway car with other people in it is usually safer than an empty one.

Let's leave the "getting around" behind and begin to explore the city itself.

Can We See the City Now?

Did you know?

The Manhattan skyline was used to represent Oz in the 1976 movie *The Wiz* with Michael Jackson and Diana Ross.

■ ■ ■

If you come into Manhattan at nighttime, you will still see the skyscrapers because many of them are lit up.

THE SKYLINE
■ ■ ■ ■ ■ ■ ■ ■ ■ ■ ■

No one ever forgets the sight of the New York City skyline. There are many ways to see it as you come into the city. Just make sure you keep looking out the window the closer you get. Some of the best views are from the Brooklyn, Manhattan, Williamsburg, Queensboro, or Triborough bridges.

Did you know?

The elevator to the 80th floor of the Empire State Building takes less than a minute!

But that's only the beginning. There's a way to see the skyline that will *really* take your breath away—seeing it from above! You can do that by going to the observation decks of the Empire State Building or 2 World Trade Center. Even though King Kong was able to climb up the outside of the Empire State Building in the movies, you'll have to go up by elevator. There are 2 outdoor observation decks—on the 86th and 102nd floors.

There are also 2 observation decks in 2 World Trade Center, New York's tallest twins—an indoor one on the 107th floor and an outdoor one on the 110th floor. On a clear day you can see into Pennsylvania. On a cloudy day, you may find yourself actually looking *down* into the clouds!

Another great way to see Manhattan is by boat. The Circle Line Cruise goes all the way around Manhattan, under all the bridges. The guides tell you about everything you're seeing—and tell some pretty funny jokes, too. The cruise lasts 3 hours and you can buy food and drink on board.

Did you know?

The World Trade Center is so big that it has its own zip code.

■ ■ ■

Fifty thousand people work in the World Trade Center. That's more than in some whole towns!

■ ■ ■

The Hudson River is saltwater until a few miles north of the city. Then it becomes freshwater. You can take an all-day boat trip up the river, starting from Pier 81 in Manhattan.

A shorter trip is the Staten Island ferry. It goes between Staten Island and the southern tip of Manhattan. Many people like to take this ferry at night, just to see the skyscrapers all lit up.

If you're not afraid of heights, take a tram trip high over the East River to Roosevelt Island. The cars are run by electric power lines in the cables overhead. You'll get a great view of the 59th Street Bridge. It only takes 3 minutes, but you'll feel like you're gliding in the air. And it's a great way to see the New York skyline.

The Neighborhoods

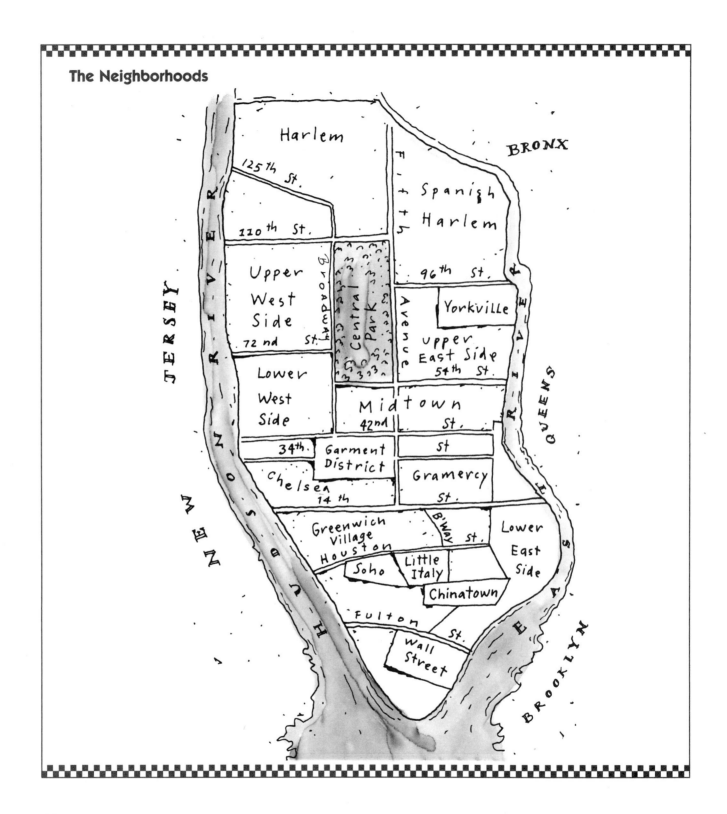

THE NEIGHBORHOODS

New York is a city of neighborhoods. People who know it well will give you directions using the names of different districts. Each of the areas has its own identity.

Midtown

Midtown, which extends from 42nd Street to 59th Street, is where most of the skyscrapers can be found. Some are so high and so close together that they make the street shady on a sunny day. There are some pretty strange ones, too: the AT&T Building has a top just like a grandfather clock, and the Chrysler Building has one like an old, shiny radiator. The old McGraw-Hill Building looks a little bit like the Empire State Building, except it's green. The Citicorp Building looks like an electric razor on stilts. The Grace Building slopes like a huge sliding pond. A building at 53rd Street and Third Avenue (called 53rd at Third) looks like a steel and glass wedding cake. And the Flatiron Building will remind you of a big wedge of cheese.

Did you know?

There's one skyscraper in midtown that has a grove of trees inside it—the IBM Building.

Look at the map of the neighborhoods. What is the area west of Central Park called?_____ What is the area at the bottom (south) of the park called?_____ If you went all the way down Broadway from the Upper West Side, you would end up in_____ _____ .

(Answers on page 130)

Midtown is also where you'll find Rockefeller Center, Times Square, F.A.O. Schwarz, the Empire State Building, the United Nations, Grand Central Terminal, and St. Patrick's Cathedral. It's also where most of the major hotels, theaters, shops, and restaurants are.

The Upper East Side

This is a quiet neighborhood of private townhouses, galleries, museums, and shops. Along Fifth Avenue (its western border), you will find many of the major museums, the most famous being the Metropolitan Museum of Art.

The Upper West Side

Separated from the Upper East Side by Central Park, the Upper West Side is the neighborhood of the famous Lincoln Center. A fountain gushes high into the sky, and around it are 4 theaters, a library, and a school for some of the most gifted young performers in the world. Every night, ballet, opera, music, and plays are performed in the buildings of Lincoln Center. The American Museum of Natural History is another highlight of this area.

Did you know?

Ever see the play or movie *West Side Story*? It took place among the playgrounds and buildings that were torn down to make Lincoln Center.

The Wall Street Area (Lower Manhattan)

As mentioned earlier, this was the first area settled in New York City. Now it's the money center of the United States, and is often called the *financial district*. Billions of dollars are made and lost each day because of the trading that happens here. Like midtown, there are many skyscrapers—including the World Trade Center. But the streets are very narrow, not like the wide, straight streets of midtown. That's because many years ago these streets were cow paths and winding dirt roads. One of the biggest attractions in this area is the South Street Seaport.

Did you know?

Until the 1800s, the Wall Street area *was* the city. Everything above it—including all of midtown—was farmland.

Those Crazy Wholesale Districts

Ever wonder where department stores get their clothes, where florists get their flowers, or where jewelers get their diamonds? Many times it's from people called wholesalers. In New York City, the wholesale districts are something to see. In the fur district, just south of Penn Station, you can see men rolling racks and racks of expensive fur coats right out on the street. In the garment district, just south of Times Square, the racks are full of clothing instead of furs. The sidewalks on Sixth Avenue between 27th and 29th Streets—the flower district—are lined with potted plants, colorful flowers, and trees so big you sometimes can't even see the street. The diamond district on West 47th Street has store after store of nothing but jewelry. It's only a block long, but it is said that about 90 percent of all the world's diamonds pass through here.

Greenwich Village and SoHo

Need a break from the huge skyscrapers in midtown? Then you may enjoy Greenwich Village. The buildings are low, the streets are lively, and there are many good restaurants and theaters.

SoHo is a strange and colorful place. The big, drab buildings used to be factories. But as you walk by them now, you'll see huge art galleries with wild paintings and sculptures. The streets are usually filled with colorfully dressed artists.

Unlike upper Manhattan, which is organized according to a grid pattern, Greenwich Village grew haphazardly—many of the streets were paved following routes of old cow paths. Even native New Yorkers sometimes get lost on these rambling streets, so bring a map.

KNOW THE NEIGHBORHOODS

1. This avenue is the western border of the Upper East Side.
2. The Wall Street area is often called the _____ district.
3. Area north of Central Park and home of the Apollo Theater
4. Name of the center in Upper West Side that takes its name from a former U.S. president
5. Wholesale district where there are many jewelry stores
6. Wholesale district where clothes are sold
7. Most skyscrapers are found here.
8. Racks of expensive fur coats are rolled right on the streets in this wholesale district.
9. This separates the Upper East Side from the Upper West Side.

(Answers on page 130)

The "Melting Pot"

When immigrants first settled in New York City, they often stuck together in their own areas. Many of these neighborhoods are still around, and when you're in them, you may feel as if you're in another country. New York City is sometimes called a *melting pot*. Like the ingredients in a big stew, the foreign people all "melt" together to form one big city.

In **Chinatown**, the narrow, winding streets are filled with restaurants, colorful banners, and markets selling vegetables you may never have seen before. The best way to experience this neighborhood is to travel along Mott Street, the main street of Chinatown. Just for fun, keep your eye out for the Chinese-style telephone booths made in the shape of pagodas.

Since the turn of the century, **Harlem** has been a center for the black people of New York City. Some of Harlem has become run-down over the years, but it is still a lively area full of shops, restaurants, theaters, clubs, and churches. Harlem's world-famous Apollo Theater, at 125th Street and Seventh Avenue, is where many black

Did you know?

Over 75 languages are spoken in New York City.

■ ■ ■

You can go into the Original Chinatown Ice Cream Factory and try some delicious red-bean ice cream.

Did you know?

Nat King Cole, James Brown, Ella Fitzgerald, and even Michael Jackson launched their careers at the Apollo.

T·R·A·V·E·L D·I·A·R·Y

We visited the _____ neighborhood and saw

_____ . Lots of _____ people

live there.

I've heard some different languages spoken in New York.

Even the English some people speak sounds different

because _____ . I want to learn to

speak _____ so I can _____ .

❖ ❖ ❖

performing artists got their start. The Apollo has been newly renovated and reopened.

There are many other interesting neighborhoods in New York—**Spanish Harlem, Little India, Little Italy**, and **Germantown**. In Brooklyn, there are Russian, Italian, and Scandinavian neighborhoods. And in Astoria, Queens, there's one of the largest Greek communities in the world.

Did you know?

You may be lucky and catch some of the festivals and parades put on by different nationalities: the Chinese New Year Festival, the San Gennaro Festival (Italian), the Puerto Rican Day Parade, the St. Patrick's Day Parade (Irish), the Greek Independence Day Parade, and many others.

Let's Get to the Good Stuff

MAJOR ATTRACTIONS

Now let's get to the stuff you came to New York to see.

The Statue of Liberty

One of New York's greatest sights to see is the Statue of Liberty, which stands 151 feet tall above her base on Liberty Island in New York Harbor. You can visit the statue by taking a ferry from Battery Park. Allow yourself at least 2½ hours for the ride and tour of Liberty Island.

The Statue of Liberty was a gift to the United States from France. A sculptor and an architect created her out of thin, beaten copper in France in the 1880s, and then took her apart and shipped her to New York in 214 separate crates.

Did you know?

The formal name of the statue is *Liberty Enlightening the World.*

MAJOR ATTRACTIONS

Can you locate the following places on the map? Color them in as you find them.

Statue of Liberty
Ellis Island
South Street Seaport
New York Stock Exchange

Rockefeller Center
St. Patrick's Cathedral
United Nations

Did you know?

Much of the money that paid for the building of the Statue of Liberty's base was raised by American school children sending in pennies, nickels, and dimes.

■ ■ ■

The tip of Lady Liberty's torch is 395 feet above sea level, and each of her eyes is 2½ feet wide.

When you arrive on Liberty Island, be prepared to climb. An elevator will take you up the base of the statue, but once you're in the statue itself, it's 168 stairs to the top!

The Statue of Liberty became a symbol to the millions of immigrants who left their homelands in the Old World to find new hope in the United States. They traveled to New York in crowded boats—many immigrants were poor and had left their homes for the first time. The statue was the first thing they saw at the end of their long, hard trip across the Atlantic Ocean, and her tall, outstretched arm became a welcoming sign of the freedom that they hoped to find. At the turn of the century, these words were added to the statue: "Give me your tired, your poor. . . ."

T·R·A·V·E·L D·I·A·R·Y

People come to New York from all over the world, both to

live and to visit. I come from _____.

My parents come from _____.

My ancestors come from _____.

I've seen people from many different countries on this trip.

Some are from:

___China

___the Philippines

___India

___Canada

___Puerto Rico

___Japan

___Australia

___France

___South America

___Ireland

❖ ❖ ❖

___Korea

___Africa

___England

___Spain

___Germany

The American Museum of Immigration, at the base of the statue, has photos, tapes, clothing, furniture, slides, films, and folk art that tell the stories of the immigrants who helped form this nation.

Did you know?

Only third-class passengers were held at Ellis Island, some for weeks and months, before they were allowed to enter the country. First- and second-class passengers were cleared where their ships anchored.

Ellis Island

You can take a ferry ride from Battery Park to Ellis Island, in New York Harbor. Between 12 and 16 million immigrants passed through here from 1892 to 1954 before being allowed to enter the United States. About half of the American population has an ancestor who was cleared through here. A 2-hour guided tour of the 30-acre island is given 4 times a day from April to November.

South Street Seaport

New York City gained much of its wealth and importance as a seaport. South Street Seaport, covering a 4-block area around Fulton Fish Market in lower Manhattan, is a tribute to the city's seafaring days. It's like a festival here all year round, with outdoor entertainers, shops, and restaurants. You

Did you know?

The South Street Seaport has one of the world's largest sailing ships. The *Peking* has 4 masts and is 376 feet long.

54

never know who or what you may run into. Street musicians play, and sometimes potters and glassblowers give demonstrations. Stop first at the visitor's information center to pick up a written guide and map. The sights are spread out over several blocks and you won't want to miss anything. On summer evenings at Pier 16, there are free concerts. If you walk to the pier, you can step onto tall sailing vessels that are almost a hundred years old. One of them, the *Pioneer*, looks like a pirate ship—and the skipper will take you out for a 2- or 3-hour sail! (You have to call in advance, though.)

Feel like going for a ride on the fastest sailing vessel in New York Harbor? Call for a reservation on the *Petrel*, which heads out of Battery Park. If you're lucky, the skipper may let you raise the sails or hold the steering wheel. It's also a great place to charter a birthday party.

Did you know?

If you take a sail on the *Petrel*, you may go along the route that the very first explorer took when he landed in New York City over 360 years ago.

New York Stock Exchange

What would you think if you walked onto a balcony, looked down, and saw a huge room crammed full of adults screaming and yelling, running around, and waving their hands wildly? If *kids* did something like that, parents would say they were making trouble, right? But the grown-ups at the New York Stock Exchange are making money. This is where the biggest companies in the country trade with each other. On this floor, fortunes are made or lost—sometimes within just 1 day!

From a balcony on the second floor you can watch the action of about 3,000 people working on the paper-littered, 90-by-90–foot floor. The walls are lined with electronic screens that show all the buying and selling activity and prices. Every sale is immediately recorded by computers and passed along by satellites to screens all over the world.

If you want to learn what all the ruckus in the Stock Exchange is about, you can either listen to a stock expert explain it in the visitors center on the third floor, take a guided tour, or walk through the exhibits on your own. The tours last 45 minutes and start every half-hour.

Rockefeller Center

Rockefeller Center is an international city within a city. Located between Fifth and Sixth Avenues, and 47th and 52nd Streets, its daily population is over 240,000 people. That's more than all but 60 U.S. cities!

You might want to start your visit at the information booth in the main lobby at 30 Rockefeller Plaza, because this center is so big, you won't know where to go. It's the largest privately owned business and entertainment complex in the world. You can find just about everything here: bookstores, drugstores, barbers, banks, movie theaters, restaurants (almost 30!), gift and clothing shops, doctors, dentists, schools, subways, and a post office. Wow!

Did you know?

John D. Rockefeller, one of the richest men in America, developed the 19 buildings on 22 acres that is called Rockefeller Center.

On the lower plaza is the famous ice-skating rink that you often see in movies. If you happen to be visiting New York City in the summer, however, you won't be able to find it. That's because the rink is made into an outdoor restaurant during the warm weather. It's a nice place to stop for lunch.

At the RCA Building, NBC gives tours all day long in their studios. You have to get your ticket the day of the tour, so it pays to get there early in the morning before they sell out. The RCA Building has an observation deck from which you can look out over the city.

In the McGraw-Hill Building, you can watch a slide show called *The New York Experience.* You'll be surrounded by movies, cartoons, and special effects in this multimedia show all about New York. Radio City Music Hall is also here. It's the largest theater in the world, and it houses the world's largest organ and chandelier. All of the buildings in Rockefeller Center are connected by an underground passageway— almost 2 miles long—that is lined with shops.

St. Patrick's Cathedral

Across Fifth Avenue from Rockefeller Center is St. Patrick's Cathedral, the largest Catholic church in the United States. Built to look like a cathedral in Cologne, Germany (in a style known as *Gothic*), its highlights include stained glass windows from France, 330-foot towers, and 30-foot pillars that support huge Gothic arches. The whole thing is made of marble and stone, and took from 1858 to 1906 to complete.

United Nations

For older kids, the United Nations Building is a fascinating place. Since 1952, this is where ambassadors from nations all over the world meet to discuss how to work together peacefully. From the Visitor's Gallery, you can listen to important meetings on headphones and switch a button to hear translations into several foreign languages. Outside is a display of many different flags of the world.

Color the flags of the United Nations.

T·R·A·V·E·L D·I·A·R·Y

I would like to be an ambassador to _____.

If I could travel to any country in the world, I would like to go to _____. I'd like to go there because _____.

If I lived in another country, I would live in _____, because _____. My favorite flag is from _____. The colors in it are _____ and it has _____ on it.

Draw the flag here.

Free tickets to various U.N. meetings are available on a first-come basis from the main information desk. If you go to a meeting, you must be quiet. There are also guided tours around the building to learn how the U.N. works. If you take a tour, don't miss the beautiful art from around the world, the moon rock, the model of *Sputnik I*, or the overhead pendulum in the Assembly lobby. You can buy gifts and postcards from around the world in the basement gift shop.

MUSEUMS

Museums were once quiet, stuffy places where kids were forced to go on school trips or Sunday outings with parents. Not any more! Many museums now have special exhibits for kids where you can take part in the show.

Metropolitan Museum of Art

The Metropolitan Museum of Art is New York City's biggest museum. Here you can see Egyptian mummies, an exhibit of arms and armor, a musical instrument gallery, and an entire section that has nothing but costumes. And there's even a Junior Museum, just for kids. You'll see special exhibits and learn how painters and craftspeople work. There's also a children's shop with toys and games, and a snack bar.

In the library of the Junior Museum you can get a written list of things to look for on your visit. These gallery hunts take you in search of objects to find and sketch, and questions to answer. It may be a beautiful

Did you know?

The 5 official languages of the United Nations are English, French, Spanish, Russian, and Chinese.

■ ■ ■

Even though the U.N. is in Manhattan, the whole complex is considered international territory. This means that when you visit the U.N., you have left New York—and the United States!

■ ■ ■

Mail a letter from the U.N. post office—they have their very own U.N. stamp.

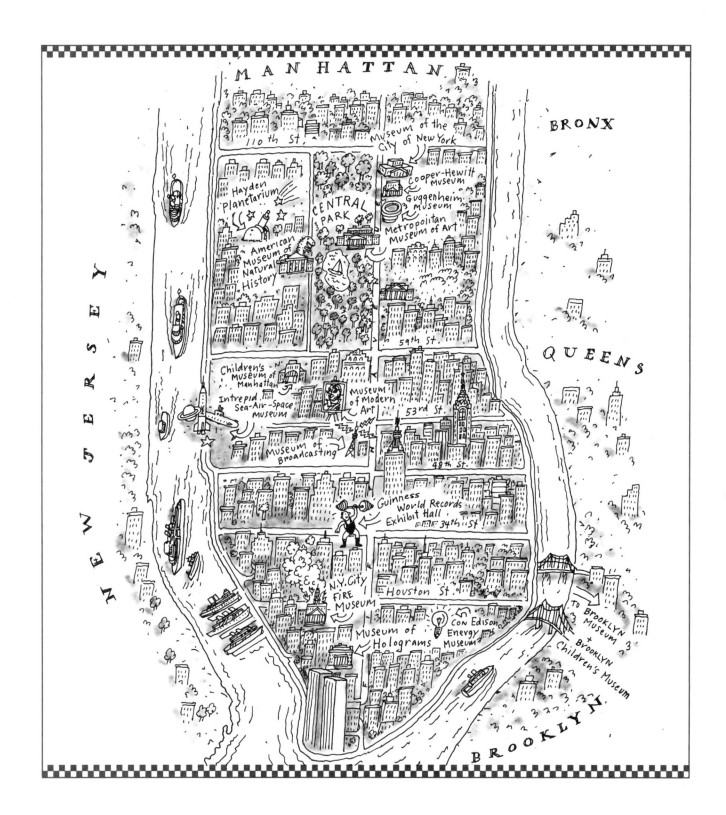

painting by Degas or Manet, or an Egyptian mummy, or even a Chinese pot you are seeking. Whatever it is, it's great fun when you look at it as a challenge.

American Museum of Natural History

Have you ever seen a real dinosaur skeleton? Well, at the American Museum of Natural History there are 7 of them! In this museum, you'll find elephants, antelopes, strange sea creatures, cave people, and even a 10-ton whale that hangs from the ceiling. Scary? Not really, because none of them are alive— some are models, and many are real but stuffed. In the 40 big rooms of this museum, you can see a parade of ancient hairy creatures called mastodons, come face-to-face with a grizzly bear, look at Indians

Did you know?

There are about 120 museums, large and small, in New York City.

■ ■ ■

Over a hundred years ago, there was to be a dinosaur museum just south of where Tavern on the Green now stands—until a crooked politician named Boss Tweed ordered that the dinosaur models be destroyed and buried under the ground. Some pieces may still be there!

T·R·A·V·E·L D·I·A·R·Y

I like _____ art. The best art I have seen is _____. I like it because

_____.

_____

If I was an artist and made something for a museum, it would

be _____.

❖ ❖ ❖

Did you know?

Dinosaurs lived on the earth for about 170 million years. They all suddenly died 65 million years ago.

inside their tepee, watch a Komodo Dragon eat a wild boar, and touch a real 34-ton meteorite that crashed to earth from outer space. In the Discovery Room, you can touch all kinds of fossils and other specimens, and on weekends there are puppet shows, music, and dance concerts.

Imagine watching a movie on a screen 4 stories high. You can do that at the Museum of Natural History, too. It's called *NatureMax*, and there are usually four different films to choose from.

Did you know?

In the American Museum of Natural History you can find stones from the moon and the Star of India, the world's largest sapphire.

■ ■ ■

At the Museum of Natural History, there's a model of a human body with see-through skin, so you can find out what's inside.

You can see all of these animals in the American Museum of Natural History.

_ _ _ _ Z Z _ _   _ _ A R

_ _ S T _ _ _ _ N

_ I _ O _ _ U _

_ _ T E _ _ P _

_ _ _ _ P _ _ _ N T

_ _ M _ D _ _ R A _ _ _ _

(Answers on page 130)

Did you know?

The projector at the Hayden Planetarium looks like a giant black space insect.

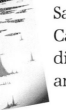

Hayden Planetarium

Next to the Museum of Natural History is the Hayden Planetarium, where you can feel what it's like to go into outer space. Here you're surrounded by nothing but stars and planets. Suddenly a comet whizzes right over your head—and you're indoors! In the Hayden Planetarium's Sky Show, you'll visit the rings of Saturn, journey into a black hole, and see the Grand Canyon of Mars. There are also special shows for different age groups, a laser show with rock music, and sometimes even live concerts.

Draw your own modern art painting.

Museum of Modern Art

The Museum of Modern Art houses a large collection of modern art masterpieces. Although they may not sound very modern, all works of art done since the end of the 1800s are considered modern art. There are sculptures, paintings, films, furniture, photographs, and drawings here. A good look at this collection will help you to see the beauty in the everyday things around you—cars, dishes, buildings, and more. If you get tired of walking around the many halls of the museum, sit down, relax, and watch a movie. Movies are shown regularly every afternoon.

Did you know?

Many of the films, particularly on Saturday and Sunday mornings, are geared to young people.

Did you know?

You can see works of art by Picasso, Klee, Mondrian, Manet, Renoir, van Gogh, and other famous artists at the Guggenheim.

Guggenheim Museum

The Guggenheim Museum is another great museum for modern art, and it's the only building in New York designed by the famous architect Frank Lloyd Wright. It's built like the shell of a snail, in a spiral, so you walk around and around from the top floor all the way to the bottom, looking at art all along the way. Don't miss the mobiles hanging from the ceiling. They are their own special kind of sculpture.

Brooklyn Museum

Here is a museum packed with history. It's the seventh-largest museum in the nation, but it's still a quiet and peaceful place right next to the Brooklyn Botanical Gardens, Prospect Park, and the zoo. The collection of ancient Egyptian art is the best outside of Cairo, Egypt, and London, England. You'll love the mummies and tombs. A lot of the things you'll see in this exhibit come from rooms inside the huge pyramids that were built to bury Egyptian royalty.

Don't miss the museum's gift shop—it's filled with dolls and dollhouse furniture, finger puppets, musical instruments, Japanese kites, and much more.

There's a great exhibit of things from the Indians of the Americas (including Eskimos). Totem poles, masks, costumes, and even a shrunken head are displayed for viewing. The collection of primitive and prehistoric art—that's the really old stuff—is world famous. And there are 28 completely furnished rooms from different times in American history. Outside, there is a sculpture garden. There are also concerts, films, talks, and special after-school programs for kids 6 to 12 years old.

Draw your favorite piece of art from your favorite museum.

Who is the artist?_____

What is the piece titled?_____

What is it made of or painted with?_____

When was it done?_____

Why do you like it?_____

_____

Museum of the City of New York

This museum is packed with fun things about the history of New York City. Take the elevator to the top floor and work your way down all 5 stories, through antique toys, model ships, dollhouses, and special New York art pieces. There are puppet shows on Saturdays from November to April, and concerts and films year-round.

Cooper-Hewitt Museum

The Cooper-Hewitt Museum is also known as the National Museum of Design. It's an old mansion that was once the home of the super-rich Carnegie family. This is the only New York branch of the Smithsonian Institution, the huge museum in Washington, D.C. The things you see here are called *decorative art*—the kinds of things made to decorate people or places, like wallpaper, furniture, glassware, metalwork, lace, and more. There are things here from all over the world and from all different periods in history.

Did you know?

The 64-room Carnegie mansion that houses the museum was the home of just one family. That's a big house!

Museums Just for Kids

There are two entire museums in New York City just for kids. One is the **Brooklyn Children's Museum**—the world's very first children's museum. You enter through the People Tube—really a huge sewer pipe—that has a stream running right down the center of it. There are lots of things to touch and play with. You'll want to join all the other kids climbing the Diamond Crystal—a jungle gym made of 75,000 plastic cubes that you can see right through.

The other museum is the **Children's Museum of Manhattan**, a nature-and-science museum where you can look at hand-cranked movies, try on costumes and makeup, climb a tree house, and see a show. Also, you can drop in any day of the summer to work on special science projects.

GULLIVER
WORLDS GREATEST
TRAVELER

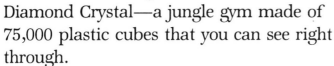

Did you know?

You can see the world's largest Raggedy Ann doll at the Guinness World Records Exhibit Hall—it's 27 feet tall!

More Museums

The **Guinness World Records Exhibit Hall** isn't just for kids, but it sure is interesting . . . especially if you're a trivia buff! Here you can see some of the biggest, smallest, and weirdest things in the world—a single hair split 14 times, the world's longest beard, and a book so small you have to see it under a microscope.

There's a museum that's in a real World War II aircraft carrier—it's the ***Intrepid* Sea-Air-Space Museum**. The ship is so big that planes used to land on it—and it still floated! Here you'll be able to feel what it's like to launch a jet fighter. You can even touch the planes that landed on the carrier and sit in the captain's chair. There's a model of a spaceship that landed on the moon, and models of some of the very first airplanes ever made.

Did you know?

The flight deck of the *Intrepid* is 900 feet long—as long as 3 football fields!

Want to go into a real navy ship? The ones docked next to the *Intrepid* have tours about once a month.

Fire engines, bright ladder trucks, big gongs—these are all found at the **New York City Fire Museum**. There are 3 floors of old firefighting equipment located in this old brick firehouse. Pay close attention to the staff—they have wonderful stories to tell.

Did you know?

There's a restaurant in Manhattan that serves only American Indian food—including buffalo steaks and blue corn chips. It's called *Silverbird*.

■ ■ ■

Many people were against electricity when it was first being used. They thought electricity gave out rays that could damage your health.

■ ■ ■

These are just a few of the things under the ground in New York City:
- subway tunnels
- TV cables
- telephone lines
- sewers
- electric cables
- gas lines
- water pipes
- steel beams to support buildings
- pedestrian walkways

At the **Museum of the American Indian**, the largest Indian museum in the world, you can see Sitting Bull's war club, the feather headdress worn by Crazy Horse, katchina dolls, totem poles, and blowguns and tomahawks. On some days there's powwow dancing and music made with ancient instruments.

At the **Con Edison Energy Museum** you'll get a free comic book. But better than that, you'll actually see what goes on underneath the New York City streets. There are plenty of surprises down there. It's fun to push and pull the knobs and levers to make the exhibits work. Here you'll learn all about energy, from the very first light bulb to solar energy to the space-age fuel cell.

If you've never seen a hologram, check out the unique **Museum of Holograms**. What are holograms? They look like real people or things, they move when you move, they look at you, and you can walk all around them. But if you try to grab one, you get nothing but air. They're special kinds of pictures made by laser beams.

Find your way out of the underground maze.

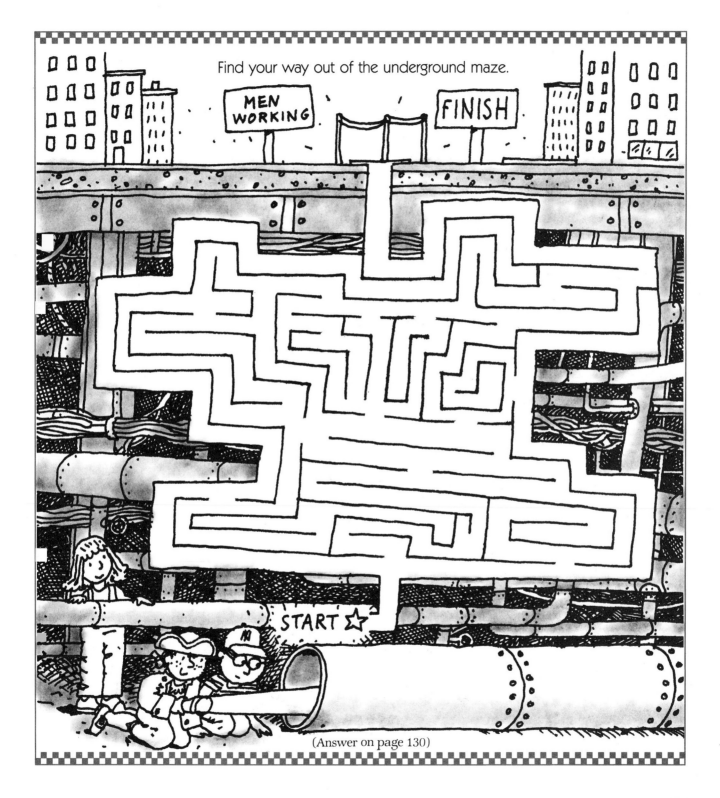

MEN WORKING

FINISH

START ☆

(Answer on page 130)

Did you know?

Lots of movies and TV shows film right on the streets of New York City. So look out for cameras—and wave!

If you love TV, go to the **Museum of Broadcasting**. It's the only place in America where you can see any TV show ever made! There are 10,000 shows to choose from—you can even see what was playing on the day you were born. There are also special exhibits and film programs to attend.

You will think you've traveled in a time machine when you visit **Richmondtown Restoration**, a life-size model of an old American town. It's in the middle of Staten Island, and is made up of buildings from the seventeenth, eighteenth, and nineteenth centuries. People are dressed in costumes from those years, and they work just like people did back then. You can see them making pottery, weaving, printing, doing leatherwork, and more. Ask for a brochure so you can find the different historic buildings. Visit the

T·R·A·V·E·L D·I·A·R·Y

My favorite old building in Richmondtown is the

_____, because _____

_____. If I was alive back then, I

would have worked as a _____.

Of all the museums I visited on this trip, I like the

_____ best. It's full of

_____. The best thing about it

is _____. If I could have my own

museum, I would call it _____,

and inside I would have a collection of _____.

❖ ❖ ❖

crafts shops, the general store, cooperage, cottages, and the oldest schoolhouse in America. Can you imagine going to school here? This is a great place to have a picnic, too.

IN SEARCH OF ANIMALS AND NATURE

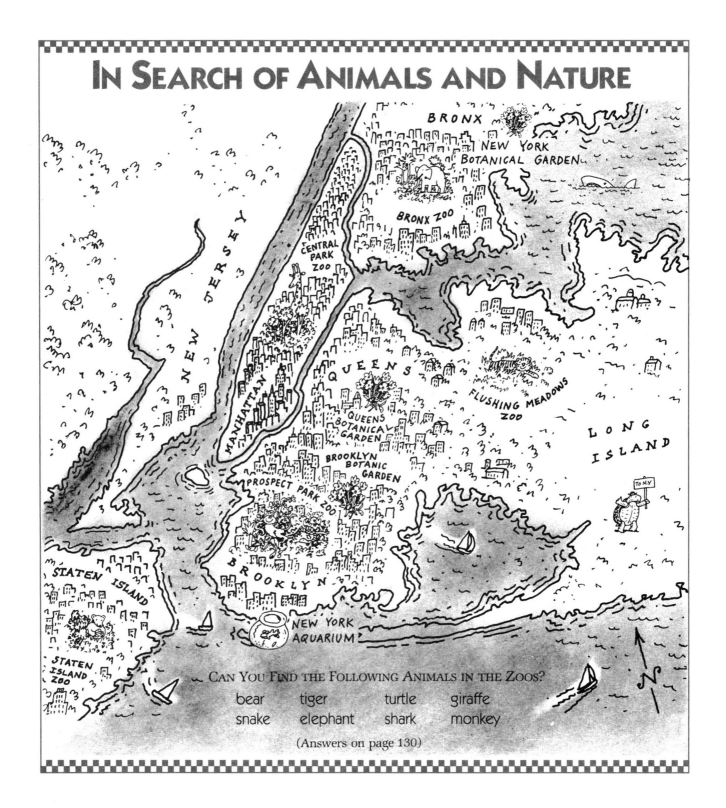

CAN YOU FIND THE FOLLOWING ANIMALS IN THE ZOOS?

bear	tiger	turtle	giraffe
snake	elephant	shark	monkey

(Answers on page 130)

ANIMALS

■ ■ ■ ■ ■ ■ ■ ■

If you like zoos, you're in luck. There's one zoo in each borough.

Bronx Zoo

The Bronx Zoo is the largest city zoo in America, and it's open every day of the year. Not only that, but on 3 days of the week—Tuesday, Wednesday, and Thursday—admission is free.

Want to see an ostrich? Want to go through a wild Asian jungle on a monorail and spot elephants and tigers? How about visiting a tropical rain forest, where birds fly free? You can do all of this at the Bronx Zoo. There are 4,150 animals here, from huge rhinoceroses to the tiniest insects.

Did you know?

In many of the Bronx Zoo exhibits, there are no cages between you and the animals—but there are moats.

■ ■ ■

The Bronx Zoo's smallest exhibit is only one square foot—it's for insects.

■ ■ ■

In 1986 alone, 772 animals were born in the Bronx Zoo.

Both indoor and outdoor exhibits show animals in their natural homes. In addition to Wild Asia, there's the Himalayan Highlands Habitat, where snow leopards and other animals live in an area just like Asian mountaintops. An indoor Jungle World has swinging monkeys, laughing birds, big turtles—there's even a rain forest with man-made clouds, and

Name a zoo or aquarium animal starting with the letter *a*, then *b*, *c*, *d*, and so on through the alphabet. Are there some letters without animals?

A _____	N _____
B _____	O _____
C _____	P _____
D _____	Q _____
E _____	R _____
F _____	S _____
G _____	T _____
H _____	U _____
I _____	V _____
J _____	W _____
K _____	X _____
L _____	Y _____
M _____	Z _____

(Examples on page 131)

a 40-foot waterfall. From there you can enter the zoo's World of Darkness, where you'll see nighttime animals like bats and foxes. You won't want to miss the World of Birds, the African Plains, the Giraffe Building, the Reptile House, the Aquatic Bird House, the Great Ape House, or the North American Exhibit.

But the best is yet to come. Visit the Children's Zoo to really find out how animals live. You can sit on a bird nest that's your size, climb a giant spiderweb, or go through a hollow log and a prairie dog tunnel. You can jump with a bullfrog or crawl inside a giant snail shell. And if that's not enough, try on a turtle shell, ride a slide down the inside of a hollow tree, smell a skunk (yuk!), or try on a pair of giant fox ears!

Did you know?

Over 3 million kids have visited the Bronx Zoo's Children's Zoo since it opened in 1981.

T·R·A·V·E·L D·I·A·R·Y

My favorite animal is the _____ because _____. It looks like _____. Some of the most _____. If I unusual animals I saw were _____ could take an animal home from the zoo with me, I'd choose _____. a _____ because _____ If I could be any kind of animal I wanted, I would be a _____ and my name would be _____

❖ ❖ ❖

Did you know?

The Central Park Zoo is the oldest zoo in the United States.

■ ■ ■

The Staten Island Zoo has one of the largest and best collections of reptiles in the United States.

■ ■ ■

An electric eel can make enough electricity to light a house. Hard to believe? A meter on the eel tank at the aquarium will show you.

There are other zoos in New York City. They are smaller than the Bronx Zoo, but still lots of fun. You can find them in Central Park, Prospect Park, Flushing Meadows–Corona Park, and Staten Island.

New York Aquarium

There's a place in Coney Island where you can come face-to-face with a shark—and live! It's the shark tank at the New York Aquarium. The aquarium's exhibits include walruses, whales, black-footed penguins, blue lobsters, octopuses, and fish from the Bermuda Triangle. You can watch sea lions perform for the crowd and dolphins sail through the air, or go to the Children's Cove where you can touch starfish, sponges, and horseshoe crabs.

PARKS AND GARDENS
■■■■■■■■■■■■■■■■■■■■■■■■

Central Park

Right in the middle of crowded Manhattan is a huge park—over ½ mile wide and 2½ miles long. Thousands of New Yorkers come here every day. Why? Because there is something for everyone to do. You can travel on pedestrian paths, bridle paths, and sunken roadways. Wandering around the park you'll see lots of runners, bike riders, roller skaters, horseback riders, and walkers enjoying the open space. Look for the hundred-year-old dairy that is now the Park Information Center. There you can find out all the different things you can do in the park.

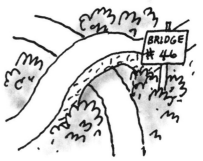

Did you know?

None of the paths in the park ever meet at an intersection. This is because there are over 46 different bridges wherever paths cross.

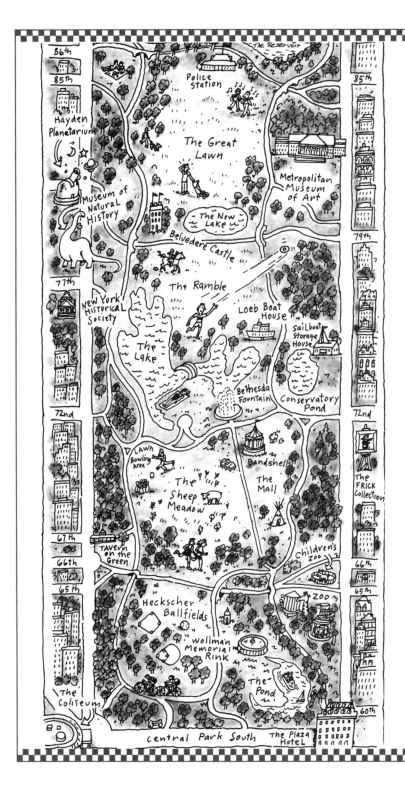

There is so much to do in Central Park that you could spend the entire day here and not see it all. Can you find the following things in this map?

family on a picnic
horseback rider
joggers
wandering musicians
paddleboat
Frisbee
sunbather
dog walker

(Answers on page 131)

CENTRAL PARK

You can watch other people play sports and games, like tennis, croquet, checkers, chess, and Frisbee, or you can play games yourself in any one of the many playing fields. At the Claremont Riding Academy you can watch talented equestrians riding over jumps, or you can rent your own horse or pony. If you like to look at animals, visit the bird sanctuary and zoo. There's even a special children's zoo where you can pet the animals. There are ponds and lakes throughout the park where you can watch hobbyists sail motorized model boats, or you can rent a paddleboat or rowboat at the Loeb Boathouse for a cruise along the lake. There are even two ice-skating rinks in the winter. In the summer you can swim at the Lasker Pool Rink.

Did you know?

There's a 3,500-year-old Egyptian monument in Central Park. It's called *Cleopatra's Needle*.

■ ■ ■

Central Park didn't always look like it does now. Before the 1860s, it was mostly swampland.

■ ■ ■

It took 3,000 workers 20 years to make Central Park. Most of the trees aren't wild; they were planted.

If you want to be entertained, there are plays and concerts. Go to the Central Park Mall to watch the street musicians, or the Delacorte Theater for the summer Shakespeare series. At the Marionette Theater you can watch puppet shows. And at the Hans Christian Andersen statue you can listen to storytellers in the summer.

While you're out exploring the park, climb on the Alice in Wonderland statue or the huge rock at Belvedere Castle. If you like merry-go-rounds, don't miss a ride on the antique Victorian carousel. And that's just part of what there is to do in the park. No matter what you like to do, Central Park has something for you.

More Parks

If you're in Brooklyn, **Prospect Park** is the place to go. There's an ice-skating rink in the winter, a zoo, a carousel, and even a children's farm. Some of the best things about this park are the special events, like a Halloween costume party (complete with a walk along the "haunted ravine"), a New Year's Eve "family night," and a birthday party for Eeyore at the children's farm.

In Queens, **Flushing Meadows–Corona Park** has an ice-skating rink, a zoo, a carousel, and a children's farm—plus the Unisphere, a hollow, 140-foot-high world globe made of steel.

T·R·A·V·E·L D·I·A·R·Y

My favorite park in New York is _____,
because _____. Central Park
is the _____ park I've ever seen. We got around the
park by _____. The best thing in Central Park
is _____. I saw people _____
_____.

❖ ❖ ❖

Color the picture any way you like.

New York Botanical Garden

You wouldn't expect to find miles of lush, beautiful flower gardens right in the heart of New York City. But there are, in 3 different boroughs. The New York Botanical Garden in the Bronx is one of the largest botanical gardens in America. It covers over 250 acres, including the 40-acre Hemlock Forest—the only woodland left uncut since the days of Indians. Here you can see New York City the way the explorers saw it. The best time to go to the New York Botanical Garden is in the spring, when flowers stretch out all around you. Indoors, you can see an African *and* an American desert and take the Skywalk over a waterfall and a make-believe volcano. If you're going to be in New York for a couple of months, you can take classes in the new Children's Garden.

Did you know?

There are over 50 different types of roses in the New York Botanical Garden's rose garden.

■ ■ ■

Scientists from the New York Botanical Garden are trying to help find the cure for cancer—in plants!

Brooklyn Botanic Garden

The Brooklyn Botanic Garden is smaller but just as beautiful. It's also easier to get to. Every spring there is a famous Cherry Blossom Festival, but all year long you can visit the authentic Japanese Garden. Here you'll find a lake that has turtles and goldfish, and an actual Japanese teahouse. Then get your nose ready—the Fragrance Garden for the Blind has the best-smelling flowers around. The Children's Garden is open to kids from the ages of 9 to 17. Here you can even learn how to garden.

Queens Botanical Garden

The Queens Botanical Garden was originally part of the 1939 World's Fair. Reopened in 1963, it has a bee garden where honey is made, and the largest wild bird shelter in New York. In the springtime, you can see 50,000 different-colored tulips in bloom.

What is Gulliver growing in his garden?

1. It's good in coleslaw _____

2. They're good sliced on sandwiches and in salads _____

3. They're good baked or fried _____

4. Rabbits and horses like to eat them _____

5. Popeye's favorite food _____

(Answers on page 131)

SPORTS

Spectator Sports

New York has teams in all the major American sports, and it's easy to get to their stadiums by subway, bus, or taxi. There is at least one major sporting event every week of the year! That's a lot of sports. In the summer and fall, you can go to Queens to watch the Mets play in Shea Stadium, which is near LaGuardia Airport. Or you can take a trip to the Bronx to see the Yankees in Yankee Stadium. New York's soccer team, the Cosmos, play in New Jersey's Meadowlands.

For winter sports fans, there's even more to do. New York's two football teams, the Giants and the Jets, are just across the Hudson River in New Jersey. The Islanders, one of New York's ice hockey teams, can be found at the Nassau Veterans Memorial Coliseum in Long Island. The Knicks (basketball) and the Rangers (ice hockey) are the only New York teams that play in Manhattan. They're at Madison Square Garden, which is just a couple of blocks away from the Empire State Building.

Did you know?

One of New York City's most popular sports is the New York City Marathon, which takes place each fall. Twenty thousand runners enter, and the ones who finish go through all 5 boroughs and over 5 bridges.

But there's more. The U.S. Open is held at Flushing Meadows–Corona Park in Queens during the first two weeks of September. For 13 days you can see the top tennis players in the world—but tickets usually must be reserved months in advance.

The one spot in New York where you can see spectacular events as different as a rodeo and a rock concert is Madison Square Garden. Check with their information center for the current calendar of events. You could see ice-skating, boxing, wrestling, horse shows, track meets, the circus, or any number of concerts.

Did you know?

In the 5 boroughs, there are over 500 parks; 900 playgrounds; 700 baseball, football, and soccer fields; 1,000 basketball courts; 35 outdoor swimming pools; and 7 skating rinks.

If you want to have fun playing sports yourself instead of just watching, New York is loaded with swimming pools, ball courts and fields, running and biking paths, ice rinks, riding stables, parks, and beaches for you to use. Call the recreation office in your borough for information and locations. No matter what the sport, New York has it.

T·R·A·V·E·L D·I·A·R·Y

My favorite sports team is_____. They come

from_____, and they play_____.

My favorite sports star is_____, who is

a_____ for_____.

The sports I like to play are_____,

but my favorite is_____. I play it at

_____with_____. I'm best at

_____.

If I could be a professional athlete, I would be a

_____.

❖ ❖ ❖

Name all the sports you can think of that you play with a ball.

_____

_____

_____

_____

_____

_____

(Answers on page 131)

Ice-Skating

Smack in the middle of midtown Manhattan is the famous **Rockefeller Center Skating Rink.** During the hot weather it's an outdoor restaurant. But every winter, the tables are cleared away, the ice is poured, and the fun begins. The best time to skate is in December, when a 7-story-tall Christmas tree glitters over the rink.

In Central Park there are two outdoor rinks, the **Wollman Memorial Rink** and **Lasker Pool Rink.** Both are owned by the city.

Manhattan has only one indoor ice-skating rink—but it's a good one. On the top floor of a building at 450 West 33rd Street, the **Sky Rink** makes you feel as if you're gliding above the city. And you are. The rink is Olympic-sized and temperature-controlled, and you can skate year-round. Serious and competitive skaters, young and old, can be found practicing their figures, dance, and hockey moves. You can even have your birthday party in the snack bar, which has a great view of the Empire State Building. The rink can provide the food, party favors, and cake.

Horseback Riding

Claremont Riding Academy is a big surprise. On the outside, it looks like a run-down old apartment building. But on the inside, it's Manhattan's only stable, and the oldest continuously running stable in the country. There are about a hundred horses here, and you won't be able to imagine where they keep them all. You can take lessons or rent a horse to ride in Central Park. Claremont offers a summer riding camp and also has shows and events. Many famous New York television and movie stars have learned to ride here.

There are a couple of other places to ride horses in New York City: **Van Cortlandt Stables** in the Bronx and **Clove Lakes Stables** in Staten Island. At Clove Lakes Stables you can even take a hayride. The stables are in a park, so after the ride you can feed the farm animals or have a picnic by an open fireplace.

The Beaches

If it's summertime and the city is getting too hot for you, hop on the subway to Orchard Beach in the Bronx, Rockaway Beach or Jacob Riis Park in Queens, or Manhattan Beach, Brighton Beach, or Coney Island in Brooklyn. (For the Orchard and Manhattan beaches and Jacob Riis Park you'll have to take a subway *and* a bus.)

Did you know?

Coney Island was in its heyday during the 1920s. Although much of the boardwalk is neglected, a walk along the beach recaptures the flavor of this once-bustling resort.

Coney Island is the site of New York's most popular beach and amusement park. More than 1½ million people visit this 3½-mile Brooklyn beach and 3-mile boardwalk on a hot summer day. Coney Island used to be a fashionable seaside resort. The Astroland amusement park then had Ferris wheels, carousels, roller coasters, and all kinds of entertainment. Today

93

most of the rides are closed and abandoned. But you can still ride the famous Cyclone roller coaster and eat hotdogs at Nathan's. Tuesday nights—in the summer—you can watch fireworks from the boardwalk.

Rockaway Beach is the biggest city beach in the country and it has a boardwalk amusement park, too. Because this is the only ocean-facing beach in New York, it has the largest waves.

If you want to *really* get away from the city, **Jones Beach** in Nassau County is one of the biggest beaches around—6½ miles long. Along the boardwalk there are 2 pools, playgrounds, restaurants, miniature golf, and a roller rink. The best way to get there, however, is by car.

Did you know?

There are 7½ miles of beach and 5½ miles of boardwalk for your enjoyment in Rockaway.

■ ■ ■

Jones Beach has a theater on a bay—the stage is separated from the audience by water.

MUSIC AND DANCE

Every summer the New York Philharmonic has free outdoor concerts in Central Park, where you can have a picnic while listening to beautiful music. The first concert of the season is always the best because it ends with fireworks. At the South Street Seaport, you can hear sea chanteys, country and western music, bluegrass, and jazz. And in Brooklyn, you can attend the outdoor concerts given by the Brooklyn Philharmonic.

Lincoln Center

If you've never been to a symphony or a ballet, here's your chance. You can listen to fine music and watch famous dancers in one of the many buildings of Lincoln Center.

Did you know?

You can see the *Nutcracker Suite* ballet every Christmas at the New York State Theater. Children from all over audition for the various parts of soldiers, mice, snowflakes, and candy canes.

Avery Fisher Hall is the home of the New York Philharmonic. The **New York State Theater**, on the south side of Lincoln Center, is the home of the New York City Opera, where you will see stories sung and acted out to classical music. The New York City Ballet

THAT'S ENTERTAINMENT

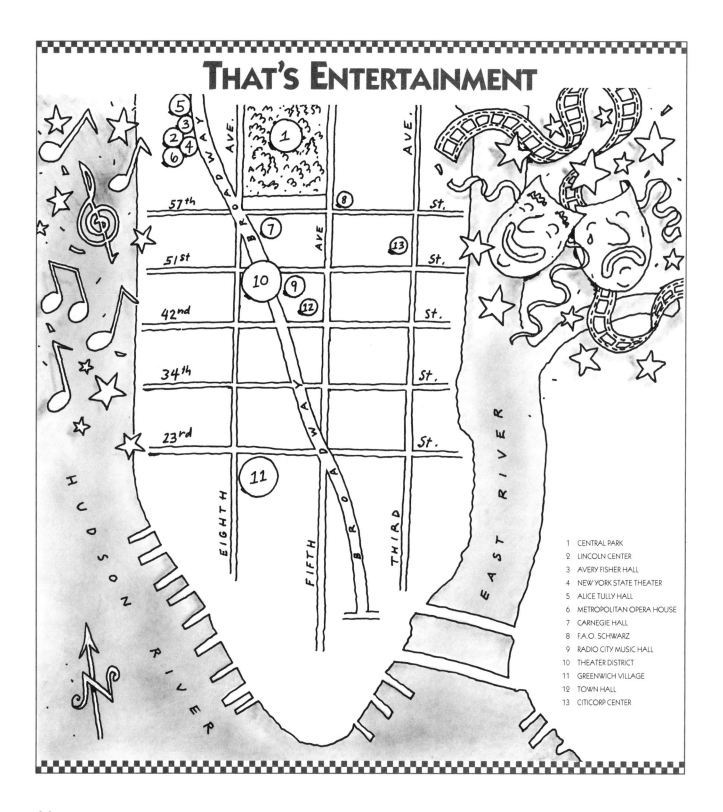

1 CENTRAL PARK
2 LINCOLN CENTER
3 AVERY FISHER HALL
4 NEW YORK STATE THEATER
5 ALICE TULLY HALL
6 METROPOLITAN OPERA HOUSE
7 CARNEGIE HALL
8 F.A.O. SCHWARZ
9 RADIO CITY MUSIC HALL
10 THEATER DISTRICT
11 GREENWICH VILLAGE
12 TOWN HALL
13 CITICORP CENTER

Alice Tully Hall is connected with the world-famous Julliard School, where some of the best classical musicians study their art.

■ ■ ■

A few years ago Carnegie Hall was going to be torn down. But New Yorkers worked to save it because of its importance in the history of New York.

also performs at the New York State Theater. Some of the best dancers in the country dance here. The Chamber Music Society of New York plays classical music at **Alice Tully Hall**. Chamber music is similar to what symphonies play, but there are fewer instruments and musicians in the group. The building in the middle of Lincoln Center is the **Metropolitan Opera House**. Even if you don't go to an opera here, the building is worth seeing. It is grand, with large pillars and beautiful murals.

You can also hear classical, jazz, and other music at **Carnegie Hall,** on West 57th Street. Many different famous groups from around the world play here. Over the years, music-related shops have opened up around this area. If you want to shop for music or musical instruments, this is a great place to visit.

Name the musical instruments.

1. _____

2. _____

3. _____

4. _____

5. _____

6. _____

(Answers on page 131)

Music Just for Kids

Some famous groups put on special shows just for kids. In the **New York Philharmonic Young People's Concerts**, not only do you hear live music, but the conductor will turn and talk to you about it. You'll learn about all the instruments and discover what makes music magical. This is one of the country's top orchestras, and the concerts are very popular, although there are only 4 of them each year. Tickets are hard to get. The best way is to show up the day of the performance and ask if there are empty seats. It's a good idea to double-check the date and time of the performance.

You may have heard a live orchestra before—but was the conductor dressed as an astronaut? Or were there magic carpets flying around? Or was a magician doing tricks? **The Little Orchestra Society—Happy Concerts for Young People**, for kids 6 to 13, is a great way to learn about music and have fun. There are 2 concerts each Saturday held at Avery Fisher Hall in Lincoln Center.

Did you know?

Sometimes almost 3,000 kids are in the audience of the Young People's Concerts.

Other special music and dance concerts for kids are performed at **Symphony Space** and the **Third Street Music School Settlement** in Manhattan, the **Brooklyn Academy of Music**, and the **Staten Island Children's Museum**. The Third Street Settlement also has a summer arts day camp.

Did you know?

At the Third Street Music School Settlement, kids as young as 2½ can start learning to play musical instruments.

T·R·A·V·E·L D·I·A·R·Y

If I played an instrument in an orchestra, I would play the
_____.
_____, because _____
Classical music sounds _____. I have heard classical
music before at _____. The places
orchestras play are _____. The biggest music
hall I've seen is _____.

❖ ❖ ❖

THEATER

Broadway

Have you ever heard of a "Broadway play"? It is a play that is put on in any one of the over 30 theaters around Broadway, Sixth, Seventh, and Eighth Avenues—in the area known as *Times Square*. The huge and colorful signs above the theaters are a show in themselves. Many of the very famous and popular plays start here before they go to other cities and countries. The most successful plays often stay in the same theater for months, and even years. It is not uncommon to see famous movie and TV actors on stage in Broadway plays. These plays usually cost a lot of money to put on because the costumes and stage set are so grand. Because of this, tickets are expensive. You can see what's playing on Broadway in many New York City newspapers and magazines.

There are many other places to see plays. Over 20 theaters are called *Off Broadway*. They put on plays to smaller audiences and are just outside the Broadway area. Even smaller and lesser-known plays are performed in over a hundred theaters all around New York City. Many of these are called *Off Off Broadway*, because they are farther away from Broadway, are not huge productions, and are often experiments in new theater ideas.

T·R·A·V·E·L D·I·A·R·Y

I think Times Square is_____. There are

so many theaters there. I've seen the play_____.

It was about_____.

I thought it was_____.

If I was an actor/actress in a play, I would be in_____

and play a_____. My costume would be

_____.

❖   ❖   ❖

Radio City Music Hall

Radio City Music Hall is the largest indoor theater in the United States. It is also famous for its design and decoration, which is called *Art Deco*. This style was popular in the 1920s and 1930s, and commonly uses big lines and rectangles, weird colors, and plastics (which were new back then). All kinds of special events come here. Some of the spectacular stage shows even have live animals on stage.

Most of the plays and shows in New York City are for adults, but kids often go to them, too. If you want to see a show that's just for kids, read on.

Theater Just for Kids

There are at least 17 groups devoted to entertaining kids. They produce plays, puppet and magic shows, story hours, musical performances, and dance shows. A good way to keep up-to-date on current entertainment is to check the Friday and Sunday New York newspapers.

Did you know?

The Rockettes, New York's famous kickline dancers, make their home at Radio City Music Hall. If you're in New York over the Christmas holidays, don't miss the tremendous show. It's unforgettable!

Did you know?

When you get a mailing from the Paper Bag Players, it comes in a brown paper bag, not an envelope!

■ ■ ■

There are many kids who are professional actors and models in New York. Some of them even make more money than their parents!

The **Paper Bag Players** put on some of the funniest shows around. They're mainly for 3- to 9-year-olds, but even adults like to join in the fun. Almost everything in the shows is made of paper bags and cardboard—yellow buses, giant shoes, costumes, even wigs! The actors have such a good time that they'll let you sing along with them. You can see them at a theater called *Symphony Space*, on Broadway at 57th Street.

In a quiet little courtyard in Greenwich Village, you'll find the **Little People's Theater Company**. From September through June, this company performs fairy tales and original shows for ages 3 to 8. If you're having your birthday in New York City, this is the place to do it. If you call in advance, you can have a party on the stage after the show.

Draw a play. Put in the scenery and all the actors in costume. What's your play called?

PRESENTING

PRODUCED
BY

If you're a little older—anywhere from second to ninth grade, then you'll enjoy the **Performing Arts Repertory Theater** or **PART**. This is an award-winning professional company that puts on musicals about Martin Luther King, Teddy Roosevelt, Sherlock Holmes, and many others. Some of the actors in this company have gone on to become Broadway and TV stars. But that's not all—PART also has magic shows. The company tours all around, but when they're in New York, they perform at the Promenade Theater, Town Hall, and the Brooklyn Academy of Music.

Do you like rock musicals? You can see one at the **Fourth Wall Repertory Company**, which also puts on comedies that take a look at what's happening in the world around us.

Central Park is the place to see puppets and marionettes. There you'll find a little cottage, the **Marionette Theater,** and its companion, the **Heckscher Puppet House.** Because the theaters are small, you need to call for reservations at both places.

The **Puppet Playhouse** at the Murphy Center is a great place for puppet shows by well known groups like the Gramercy Puppet Theater. If you're in midtown on any weekday, you can see a show at **F.A.O. Schwarz**. If you're in midtown on a Saturday, head over to the **Citicorp Center** for Kid's Day. There you'll see puppet shows and clowns and listen to storytellers.

SHOPPING

New York City is famous for having some of the biggest and best stores in America—and that goes for kids' stores, too!

Toys

F.A.O. Schwarz is the number one toy store for kids in New York. You'll see the best collection of stuffed animals anywhere—including giraffes that are as tall as the ceiling! Huge model trains chug along wide tracks, and even full-size log cabins are for sale. Interested in a motorized car just big enough for a kid? That's there, too. A lot of this stuff is way too expensive to buy, but you'll love looking at it. On weekday afternoons, they even have a puppet show.

T·R·A·V·E·L D·I·A·R·Y

The best toy store I've ever been to was _____.

The best thing they had was a _____.

I bought _____.

My favorite toys are _____.

I have _____.

Its color is _____. I _____ with it.

If I could buy any toy I wanted, it would be _____,

because _____.

❖ ❖ ❖

Did you know?

The world's *largest* department store is in New York City—and a big sign on the side of Macy's tells you so.

Toy Park isn't as fancy as F.A.O. Schwarz, but it's bigger. In fact, it probably has the largest choice of brand-name toys in the city. **The Last Wound-Up** has two small stores, but they're both chock-full of music boxes and other toys that wind up.

Has your favorite doll's head fallen off? Is the stuffing coming out of one of your animals? Take it to the **New York Doll Hospital**, where dolls have been repaired since 1900.

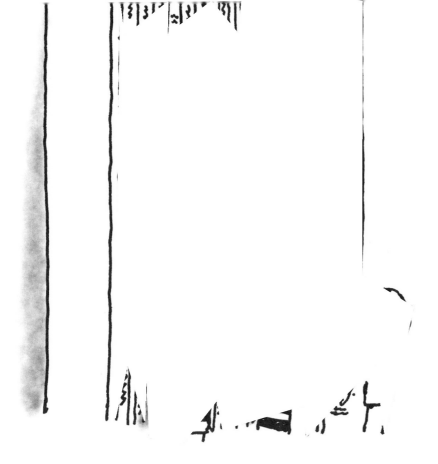

Books, Records, and Tapes

The biggest selection of children's books and videotapes is at B. Dalton's Fifth Avenue store. Barnes & Noble Sale Annex, Doubleday, and the Classic Book Shop have a lot, too.

But the bookstores that are the most fun are the ones *just* for kids. **Eeyore's Books for Children** is one of the best. It has two locations in Manhattan. Look for special events and story hours. There's even an annual story-writing contest.

Books of Wonder has a terrific selection of books. Not only is it the largest children's bookstore in New York, but it's different than most of the others. First of all, it has hundreds of very old and rare books with

Did you know?

New York City stores sell 10 billion dollars' worth of goods each year.

Write a letter to the author or illustrator of your favorite book.

Dear

beautiful illustrations. Also, it specializes in *The Wizard of Oz*. Here you'll find every book ever written about Oz, including some signed by the author himself. There's an Oz exhibit, and plenty of Oz gifts other than books.

If there's anything you need to find in records, tapes, or CDs, chances are **Tower Records** has it. There are two stores in Manhattan, but the one downtown is bigger. Music videos play all around you while you shop.

T·R·A·V·E·L D·I·A·R·Y

I read _____ books a month. My favorite book is _____

_____. It's about _____

_____.

❖ ❖ ❖

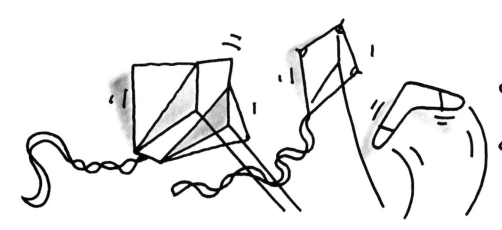

Science, Magic, and Model Trains

Believe it or not, there's a store that sells only toys you can use in the sky! At **The Silent Sky**, you can buy hot-air balloons, windmills, boomerangs, kites, and special science kits. On Saturday mornings, there is a free science workshop, where you can see experiments that test the laws of science.

You can choose from over 5,000 magic tricks at **Louis Tannen**, the world's largest magic store. The store even sponsors a summer magic camp and publishes its own magic magazine. **The Magic Towne House** sells tricks, too, and it also has great magic shows. For a truly magical birthday, you can have your party here.

If you like model trains, you'll go crazy at New York's model train store **Red Caboose**. It has everything you need—including the tiniest train parts.

DINING

There are lots of places to eat in New York City from the very simple to the very fancy. Street vendors sell hot dogs, pretzels, Italian ices, and even roasted chestnuts (a winter specialty). It's a lot of fun to grab a bite to eat from a sidewalk cart, but if you're looking for a restaurant you have tons to choose from. Every type of food and price range is available in New York City, but there are a few very special places you may want to go.

Did you know?

There is a hotdog, ice cream, pretzel, or Italian ice vendor on nearly every street corner in Manhattan. You haven't "done" New York City until you've tried a corner treat.

If you like food that's wild and different, you're in the right place because New York is loaded with restaurants that specialize in food from other lands. Chinese restaurants are in just about every neighborhood, but you can choose from dozens in Chinatown. If you like spicy food, just go to Sixth Street between First and Second Avenues—there's a

different Indian restaurant in almost every building. All you spaghetti lovers will feel as if you're in heaven on Mulberry Street in Little Italy. And for good Greek food, take a subway ride to Astoria, Queens. There you can have dinner at Roumeli and dessert at Omonia Cafe. (If you have a sweet tooth, don't miss their *Ek mek Kataifi*.)

"Oh, Mamma likes children!" That's what a manager of **Mamma Leone's** says about the famous family restaurant in Times Square. Crazy decorations are all over the place, and kids get free balloons. Make sure you're really hungry when you eat here—you get a plateful of vegetables, Italian bread, and cheeses before you even order dinner.

A really neat place to eat is at the **Horn & Hardart Automat** in midtown. Just stick in a few quarters and your food pops out of the wall! New York used to have lots of these automats, but this is the only one left.

113

Huge banana splits and frozen hot chocolate are the specialties of **Serendipity** in Manhattan. There's also a small toy store in front.

T·R·A·V·E·L D·I·A·R·Y

While in New York, I want to eat_____.

My favorite kind of food is_____. Of all

the food I tasted here in New York so far, I liked_____

_____ the best.

Fun places I ate: What I ate there:

_____   _____

_____   _____

_____   _____

_____   _____

_____   _____

❖ ❖ ❖

If you really want to get sloppy, **Jahn's** in Queens will sell you a "kitchen sink." That's a gigantic bowl with 18 scoops of ice cream, 8 sauces, nuts, whipped cream, and toppings! But don't eat so much that you get a stomachache!

Did you know?

If you want to eat fast, don't worry—*all* your favorite fastfood places are in New York City.

■ ■ ■

While you're in the city, go to a salad bar at one of the many Korean sidewalk greengrocers. It's a treat of cold and hot food—and you can take as much as you want!

■ ■ ■

Tavern on the Green was once a sheep shelter.

Rumplemayer's is a dream restaurant. It not only has an old-fashioned soda fountain that serves ice cream, but its walls are covered with dolls and stuffed animals. It's a fancy place, so you'll have to dress up.

For a special dress-up dinner, **Tavern on the Green** in Central Park is tops. The main dining room has glass walls and ceiling, and outside there are trees lit up with Christmas lights all year round. If it's your birthday, the waiters will even sing to you.

Are You Tired Yet?

New York City is an amazing place. There are millions of things to see and do—probably more than in any other city in the world. You'll want to come back again and again to see those places you've missed, as well as those places that are new. You can never see it all—New York is always changing.

Reading up on where you want to go will help you enjoy your trips. And your travel journal will help you remember what to tell your friends about when you get home.

For more ideas on what to do in New York City, contact a travel agent or the New York State Chamber of Commerce. Look for colorful guides and brochures at many of the museums and restaurants. A good way to find out about special events for kids is to look at the "Events" sections of the New York newspapers, particularly on Friday and Sunday. They have special lists of things for kids to do. ENJOY!

T·R·A·V·E·L D·I·A·R·Y

I've seen a lot in New York City. Some places I went to that

aren't in this book are _____.

My favorite thing to do in New York is _____.

If I come back, I will visit _____,

but I won't visit _____.

I liked _____ best because _____

_____.

When I get home, the first thing I will tell my friends is _____

_____. If I have to write about my trip for school, I

will tell my teacher about _____.

The best day of the trip was _____, because

_____.

My favorite souvenir is _____. I got it at _____.

I have everything I collected on this trip in my _____.

The next trip I take, I want to go to _____

with _____.

C·A·L·E·N·D·A·R

JANUARY

Central Park Winter Festival (212) 397-8222

Make Your Own Calendar Workshop, Metropolitan Museum of Art (212) 879-5500, ext. 3932

Original Christmas Plays, Little People's Theater Company (212) 765-9540

Radio City Music Hall Christmas Extravaganza and Giant Tree at Rockefeller Center (212) 757-3100

FEBRUARY

Black History Month Celebration, American Museum of Natural History (212) 873-1300

Chinese New Year Parade, Chinatown (212) 431-9740

Children's Purim Puppet Show Carnival, Lincoln Square Synagogue (212) 874-6100

Ice Capades, Madison Square Garden (212) 564-4400

MARCH

Birthday Party for Eeyore, Children's Farm, Prospect Park (718) 788-0055

Central Park Egg-Rolling Contest, Great Lawn, Central Park (212) 520-5331

Ringling Brothers and Barnum & Bailey Circus, Madison Square Garden (212) 564-4400

St. Patrick's Day Parade, Fifth Avenue, Manhattan (212) 397-8222

JULY

Coney Island Air Show (718) 226-1234

Macy's Fireworks Display (212) 695-4400

Fireworks: Central Park (212) 397-3100; Shea Stadium (718) 507-8499

Big Apple Circus (212) 369-5110

AUGUST

Elephant Weekend, Bronx Zoo (212) 367-1010

Macy's World's Largest Games, Manhattan (212) 560-4441

Model Aviation Day, Rockefeller Center (212) 489-4300

Out-of-Doors at Lincoln Center (212) 877-1800

SEPTEMBER

San Gennaro Festival, Mulberry Street, Little Italy (212) 226-9546

Richmondtown County Fair, Richmondtown Restoration (718) 351-9414

Brooklyn Street Fairs (718) 783-4469

New York Is Book Country (212) 661-6030

The dates and times of many of these events change from year to year. For complete information, be sure to call the phone number listed.

APRIL

The Great Egg Event, Bronx Zoo (212) 367-1010
Kite-Fly and Animal Workshop, New York Aquarium (718) 266-8500
Meadowfair, Staten Island Children's Museum (718) 273-2060
Ringling Brothers and Barnum & Bailey Circus, Madison Square Garden (212) 564-4400

MAY

Big Apple Circus (212) 369-5110
Free Summer Concerts:
Central Park (212) 580-8700;
South Street Seaport (212) 669-9400
Live Concert under the Stars, Hayden Planetarium (212) 769-5900
Ringling Brothers and Barnum & Bailey Circus, Madison Square Garden (212) 564-4400

JUNE

Central Park Storytelling Hours, Hans Christian Andersen statue, Saturdays 11:00 A.M.
Claremont Riding Academy Riding Camp (212) 724-5100
Doo-It Day, Children's Art Carnival, Damrosch Park, Manhattan (212) 234-4093
Sky Rink Summer School (212) 239-8385
Summer Aquatic Adventures, New York Aquarium (718) 266-8624
Third Street Music School Settlement Summer Program (212) 777-3240
Big Apple Circus (212) 369-5110
Zoo Olympics and Great Snakes Alive!, Staten Island Zoo (718) 442-3100

OCTOBER

Halloween Party, Bronx Zoo (212) 367-1010
Claremont Riding Academy Halloween Ride (212) 724-5100
Ghost Crabs and Goblin Sharks, New York Aquarium (718) 266-8500
The Great Pumpkin Festival, Prospect Park (718) 788-0055
Haunted Greenhouse, New York Botanical Garden (718) 220-8700
Kite Day, Central Park (212) 472-2623

NOVEMBER

Children's Book Week, New York Public Library (212) 340-0906
International Horse Show, Madison Square Garden (212) 563-8000
Macy's Thanksgiving Day Parade, Manhattan (212) 560-4441
Radio City Music Hall Christmas Extravaganza (212) 757-3100

DECEMBER

Hanukkah Party, 92nd Street YMCA (212) 427-6000, ext. 179
Christmas Show, Hayden Planetarium (212) 769-5900
Radio City Music Hall Christmas Extravaganza (212) 757-3100
Nutcracker Suite ballet at Lincoln Center (212) 877-1800
Original Christmas Plays, Little People's Theater Company (212) 765-9540
Rockefeller Center Tree-Lighting Ceremony (212) 489-4300
Sesame Street Christmas Show, Madison Square Garden (212) 564-4400
Christmas at Richmondtown, Richmondtown Restoration (718) 351-9414

A·P·P·E·N·D·I·X

Prices and times are constantly changing. To be sure of current rates and hours of operation, call the numbers listed.

AMERICAN MUSEUM OF NATURAL HISTORY   (212) 769-5100/(212) 769-5121 (*NatureMax*). Central Park West at 79th Street, Manhattan. 10:00 A.M.–5:45 P.M., Mon., Tues., Thurs., & Sun.; 10:00 A.M.–9:00 P.M., Wed., Fri., & Sat. $3.50/adult; $1.50/child. *NatureMax*: $3.25/adult; $1.50/under 17 (plus admission).

B. DALTON   (212) 247-1740. 666 Fifth Avenue (at 53rd Street), Manhattan. 8:30 A.M.–7:00 P.M., Mon.–Fri.; 9:30 A.M.–6:30 P.M., Sat.; noon–5:00 P.M., Sun.

BARNES & NOBLE SALE ANNEX   (212) 807-0099. Fifth Avenue and 18th Street, Manhattan. 9:45 A.M.–6:45 P.M., Mon.–Fri.; 9:45 A.M.–6:00 P.M., Sat.; 11:00 A.M.–5:00 P.M., Sun.

BOOKS OF WONDER (main store)   (212) 989-3270. 132 Seventh Avenue (at 18th Street), Manhattan. 11:00 A.M.–9:00 P.M., Mon.–Sat.; noon–6:00 P.M., Sun. There is also a branch at 464 Hudson Street in Greenwich Village—call (212) 989-3270.

BRIGHTON BEACH   (718) 946-1350. 15th Street to Ocean Parkway, Brooklyn. Lifeguard on duty 10:00 A.M.–6:00 P.M.

BRONX ZOO   (212) 367-1010. Bronx River Parkway at Fordham Road, the Bronx. *Mar.–Oct.*: 10:00 A.M.–5:00 P.M., Mon.–Sat.; 10:00 A.M.–5:30 P.M., Sun. & holidays. Free (Tues.–Thurs.); $3.75/adult; $1.50/under 12 (Fri.–Mon.). *Nov.–Feb.*: 10:00 A.M.–4:30 P.M., daily. Free (Tues.–Thurs.); $1.50/adult; $.75/under 12. (Fri.–Mon.). *Safari Tour Train*

(narrated tour through zoo): $1.25/adult; $1.00/under 12. *Skyfari* (aerial tramway over zoo): $1.00/adult; $.75/under 12. *Bengali Express Monorail* (narrated train through Wild Asia): $1.25/adult; $.75/under 12. *Camel rides*: $1.00.

Children's Zoo   *Apr.–Oct.*: 10:00 A.M.–5:00 P.M., Mon.–Sat. (last ticket sold at 4:00 P.M.); 10:00 A.M.–5:30 P.M., Sun. & holidays (last ticket sold at 4:30 P.M.).

BROOKLYN ACADEMY OF MUSIC PERFORMING ARTS FOR YOUNG PEOPLE   (718) 636-4130. 30 Lafayette Avenue, Brooklyn. Call for schedule and prices.

BROOKLYN BOTANIC GARDEN   (718) 622-4433. 1000 Washington Avenue, Brooklyn. *Apr.–Oct.*: 8:00 A.M.–6:00 P.M., Tues.–Fri.; 10:00 A.M.–6:00 P.M., Sat. & Sun. *Nov.–Mar.*: 8:00 A.M.–4:30 P.M., Tues.–Fri.; 10:00 A.M.–4:30 P.M., Sat. & Sun.

BROOKLYN CHILDREN'S MUSEUM   (718) 735-4432/(718) 735-4400. 145 Brooklyn Avenue, Brooklyn. 2:00 P.M.–5:00 P.M., Mon., Wed., & Fri.; 2:00 P.M.–8:00 P.M., Thurs.; 10:00 A.M.–5:00 P.M., Sat., Sun., & public-school holidays. Closed Tues. $2.00/adult; $1.00/child.

BROOKLYN MUSEUM   (718) 638-5000. 200 Eastern Parkway, Brooklyn. 10:00 A.M.–5:00 P.M., Wed.–Mon. Closed Tues. $2.00/adult; $1.00/student 12 and above with I.D.; free/under 12 & senior citizen.

CARNEGIE HALL   (212) 247-7459. 154 West 57th Street, Manhattan. Call for schedule.

CENTRAL PARK (212) 397-3100/(212) 408-0100 (Department of Parks and Recreation); (212) 360-1333 (for recorded information about free events); (212) 397-3091 (for Urban Rangers who will assist you about family events). Between 59th Street and 110th Street, and between Fifth Avenue and Central Park West, Manhattan. Open all day. For a free calendar of events, send a stamped, self-addressed envelope to: Department of Parks, 830 Fifth Avenue, New York, New York 10021.

Belvedere Castle (212) 772-0210. Middle of the park, about 79th Street. Family entertainment, May–Sept., 11:00 A.M., Sat.

Carousel (212) 879-0244. Middle of the park, off 65th Street. All year round in good weather: 10:30 A.M.–3:45 P.M., Mon.–Fri.; 10:30 A.M.–4:45 P.M., Sat. & Sun. $.50/all.

Children's Zoo (212) 408-0271. 65th Street off Fifth Avenue. 10:00 A.M.–4:30 P.M., daily. $.10/all.

Conservatory Lake 74th Street, just inside Fifth Avenue.

Diana Ross Playground Just inside 81st Street footpath at Central Park West.

Heckscher Puppet House (212) 397-3160. At the level of 62nd Street and Seventh Avenue. 10:30 A.M. (and sometimes at noon), Mon.–Fri. Call for schedule and prices.

Horse and buggy rides Horses line up at 59th Street and Fifth Avenue and at Tavern on the Green. Ask drivers for rates.

Lasker Pool Rink (212) 397-3142. Lenox Avenue and 110th Street. Noon–9:30 P.M., Wed.–Fri.; 11:00 A.M.–10:00 P.M., Sat. & Sun. Call for rates.

Marionette Theater (212) 988-9093. Just inside Central Park West (take the 81st Street footpath to enter). Shows are fall through spring, noon & 3:00 P.M., Sat. $2.00/all. Reservations required.

Pony rides Fifth Avenue and 59th Street (just below zoo). Spring through summer. Call Children's Zoo for information.

Rowboats at Loeb Boathouse (212) 517-2233. Northeast corner of the lake (off 74th Street). Spring through fall, 9:00 A.M.–5:00 P.M., Mon.–Sat. $6/hour; $20 deposit required.

Statues (Alice in Wonderland and Hans Christian Andersen). Both near Conservatory Lake.

Wollman Memorial Rink (212) 772-3862. Southeast area of park; enter at Avenue of the Americas or 65th Street. Call for hours and rates.

CHILDREN'S MUSEUM OF MANHATTAN (212) 765-5904. 314 West 54th Street (between Eighth and Ninth Avenues), Manhattan. 11:00 A.M.–5:00 P.M., Tues.–Fri.; 11:00 A.M.–5:00 P.M., Sat. & Sun. $1.00/adult; $2.00/child (Tues.–Fri.); $3.00/adult; $2.00/child (Sat. & Sun.).

CHINATOWN Between Canal and Worth Streets (east of Broadway), Manhattan.

CIRCLE LINE CRUISE (212) 563-3200. Pier 83 (the Circle Line Plaza), west end of 42nd Street, Manhattan. Apr.–Nov., daily. Call for schedule. $12.00/adult; $6.00/under 12.

CITICORP BUILDING (212) 559-2330. 53rd Street (between Lexington and Third Avenues), Manhattan.

CLAREMONT RIDING ACADEMY (212) 724-5100. 175 West 89th Street (between Amsterdam and Columbus Avenues), Manhattan. 6:30 A.M.–10:00 P.M., Mon.–Fri.; 6:30 A.M.–5:00 P.M., Sat. & Sun. Call for rates.

CLASSIC BOOK SHOP AND SALE ANNEX (212) 221-2252. 1212 Avenue of the Americas (between 47th and 48th Streets), Manhattan. 8:00 A.M.–6:50 P.M., Mon.–Fri.; 10:00 A.M.–5:50 P.M., Sat.; noon–5:50 P.M., Sun.

CLOVE LAKES STABLES (718) 543-4433. 1025 Clove Road, Staten Island. 8:00 A.M.–4:00 P.M., Mon.–Sun. Call for rates.

CON EDISON ENERGY MUSEUM (212) 460-6244. 145 East 14th Street (between Third Avenue and Irving Place), Manhattan. 10:00 A.M.–4:00 P.M., Tues.–Sat. Free.

CONEY ISLAND (718) 946-1350. Surf Avenue to West 37th Street, Brooklyn. Lifeguard on duty 10:00 A.M.–6:00 P.M.

COOPER-HEWITT MUSEUM (The Smithsonian Institution's National Museum of Design) (212) 860-6898. 2 East 91st Street (between Fifth and Madison Avenues), Manhattan. 10:00 A.M.–9:00 P.M., Tues.; 10:00 A.M.–5:00 P.M., Wed.–Sat.; noon–5:00 P.M., Sun. Closed Mon. & major holidays. $2.00/adult; $1.00/student & senior citizen; free/under 12. Tues. evenings 5:00–9:00 admission is free for everyone.

DIAMOND DISTRICT 47th Street (between Fifth and Sixth Avenues), Manhattan.

DOUBLEDAY BOOK SHOP (212) 397-0550. 724 Fifth Avenue (near 57th Street), Manhattan. 9:00 A.M.–midnight, Mon.–Sat.; noon–5:00 P.M., Sun.

EEYORE'S BOOKS FOR CHILDREN Two branches: (212) 362-0634, 2212 Broadway (between 78th and 79th Streets); and (212) 988-3404, 25 East 83rd Street (between Fifth and Madison Avenues), Manhattan. Broadway store hours: 10:00 A.M.–6:00 P.M., Mon.–Sat.; 10:30 A.M.–5:00 P.M., Sun. (summer hours for Sun.: noon–5:00 P.M.). Madison Avenue store hours: 10:00 A.M.–6:00 P.M., Mon.–Sat.; noon–5:00 P.M., Sun. (Closed Sun. July–Aug.)

ELLIS ISLAND (212) 269-5755. By ferry from Battery Park in Manhattan, or by ferry from Liberty State Park in Jersey City, New Jersey. Season: May–Oct. Call for schedule and fare.

EMPIRE STATE BUILDING (212) 736-3100, ext. 55 (observation deck). Fifth Avenue and 34th Street, Manhattan. 9:30 A.M.–midnight (last elevator is at 11:30 P.M.), daily. $3.25/adult; $1.75/under 12 & senior citizen.

F.A.O. SCHWARZ (212) 644-9400. 767 Fifth Avenue (at 58th Street), Manhattan. 10:00 A.M.–6:00 P.M., Mon.–Sat.; 10:00 A.M.–8:00 P.M., Thurs.; noon–5:00 P.M., Sun.

FINANCIAL DISTRICT South of Brooklyn Bridge (approximately Fulton Street and south), Manhattan.

FLOWER DISTRICT Avenue of the Americas (between 27th and 29th Streets), Manhattan.

FLUSHING MEADOWS–CORONA PARK (718) 699-6728/(718) 507-3000. Between Grand Central Parkway and the Van Wyck Expressway, Flushing, Queens.

Carousel (718) 592-6539. 111th Street and 54th Avenue. 10:30 A.M.–7:00 P.M., Mon.–Fri.; 10:30 A.M.–8:00 P.M., Sat. & Sun. Closed for rain. $.50/all.

Ice-skating (the New York City Building) (718) 271-1996. Wed.–Sun. in the winter. Call for schedule and fees.

Queens Zoo and Heckscher Children's Farm (718) 699-7239. 10:00 A.M.–3:45 P.M., daily. Free.

FOURTH WALL REPERTORY COMPANY (212) 222-7008. Truck and Warehouse Theater, 79 East 4th Street (near Second Avenue), Manhattan. $10.00/adult; $6.00/child.

FUR DISTRICT Seventh Avenue (between 27th and 30th Streets), Manhattan.

GARMENT DISTRICT Between Eighth and Sixth Avenues (between 41st and 34th Streets), Manhattan.

GERMANTOWN Approximately between East 79th and 86th Streets (between Park Avenue and East River), Manhattan.

GIANTS STADIUM (201) 935-8111. East Rutherford, New Jersey. Sept.–Dec. Call for schedule and ticket prices.

GRAMERCY PUPPET THEATER (212) 254-9074. Call for schedule, fees, and locations of shows.

GRAND CENTRAL TERMINAL (212) 935-3969 (tour information). 42nd Street (between Lexington and Vanderbilt Avenues), Manhattan.

GREENWICH VILLAGE Between 14th and Houston Streets (between Fifth Avenue and the Hudson River), Manhattan.

GUGGENHEIM MUSEUM (212) 860-1313. 1071 Fifth Avenue (between 88th and 89th Streets), Manhattan. 11:00 A.M.–5:00 P.M., Wed.–Sun. & holidays; 11:00 A.M.–8:00 P.M., Tues. Closed Mon., except holidays. $2.00/adult; $1.25/student and senior citizen; free/under 7. Tues. evenings 5:00 P.M.–8:00 P.M. free.

GUINNESS WORLD RECORDS EXHIBIT HALL (212) 947-2335. 350 Fifth Avenue (the Empire State Building), Manhattan. 9:30 A.M.–6:00 P.M., Mon.–Sun. $3.00/adult; $2.00/4–12 child; free/under 4.

HARLEM Between 110th and 162nd Streets (between Park and Morningside Avenues—above Morningside Park, Harlem extends all the way west to the Hudson River), Manhattan.

HAYDEN PLANETARIUM   (212) 769-5900. West 79th Street and Central Park West, Manhattan. Call for hours of operation and schedule of *Sky Show*. $3.75/adult; $2.00/2–12 child; free/under 2. (Planetarium fee covers admission to the American Museum of Natural History.)

HORN & HARDART AUTOMAT   (212) 599-1665. 200 East 42nd Street (at Third Avenue), Manhattan. 6:30 A.M.–10:00 P.M., daily.

INTREPID SEA-AIR-SPACE MUSEUM   (212) 245-0072. Pier 86, West 46th Street and the Hudson River, Manhattan. 10:00 A.M.–5:00 P.M. (last admission 4:00 P.M.), Wed.–Sun. Closed only on Christmas and New Year's Day. $4.75/adult; $4.00/senior citizen; $2.50/6–12 child; free/under 5.

JACOB RIIS PARK   (718) 474-4600. Beach 149th Street to Beach 169th Street, Queens. Lifeguard on duty 9:00 A.M.–7:00 P.M.

JAHN'S   (718) 847-2800. 117-03 Hillside Avenue (near Lefferts Boulevard), Queens. 11:30 A.M.–11:30 P.M., Mon.–Thurs.; 11:30 A.M.–1:00 A.M., Fri. & Sat.; noon–11:30 P.M., Sun.

JONES BEACH STATE PARK   (516) 785-1600. Wantagh, Long Island. Lifeguard on duty 8:00 A.M.–7:00 P.M.

THE LAST WOUND-UP   (212) 787-3388. 290 Columbus Avenue (between 74th and 75th Streets), Manhattan. 10:00 A.M.–8:00 P.M., Sun.–Thurs.; 10:00 A.M.–10:00 P.M., Fri. & Sat.

LINCOLN CENTER   (212) 877-1800, ext. 424. Broadway (between 62nd and 66th Streets), Manhattan.

LITTLE INDIA   East 6th Street (between Second and First Avenues), Manhattan.

LITTLE ITALY   The area north of Chinatown (between Mulberry Street and the Bowery, and between Canal and Spring Streets), Manhattan.

LITTLE ORCHESTRA SOCIETY—HAPPY CONCERTS FOR YOUNG PEOPLE   (212) 704-0840. Lincoln Center (West 65th Street and Broadway), Manhattan; Avery Fisher Hall (concerts for 5- to 12-year-olds), or Bruno Walter Auditorium (concerts for 3- to 5-year-olds). Call for schedule and ticket information.

LITTLE PEOPLE'S THEATER COMPANY   (212) 765-9540. 39 Grove Street (between Bedford and Bleecker Streets), Manhattan. Call for schedule. $5.00/all.

LOUIS TANNEN   (212) 239-8383. 6 West 32nd Street (between Fifth and Sixth Avenues), Fourth Floor, Manhattan. 9:00 A.M.–5:30 P.M., Tues., Wed., & Fri.; 9:00 A.M.–7:00 P.M., Thurs.; 9:00 A.M.–3:00 P.M., Sat.

MACY'S   (212) 695-4400. 34th Street (between Broadway and Seventh Avenue), Manhattan. 9:45 A.M.–8:30 P.M., Mon., Thurs., & Fri.; 9:45 A.M.–6:45 P.M., Tues. & Wed.; 9:45 A.M.–6:00 P.M., Sat.; noon–6:00 P.M., Sun.

MADISON SQUARE GARDEN   (212) 563-8000. 4 Pennsylvania Plaza (West 34th Street and 8th Avenue), Manhattan. Call for ticket and schedule information.

MAGIC TOWNE HOUSE   (212) 752-1165. 1026 Third Avenue (between East 60th and East 61st Streets), Manhattan. Call for hours.

MAMMA LEONE'S   (212) 586-5151. 239 West 48th Street (between Broadway and Eighth Avenue), Manhattan. 11:30 A.M.–2:30 P.M. (lunch and buffet), 3:30 P.M.–11:30 P.M. (dinner), Mon.–Fri.; 12:30 P.M.–11:30 P.M., Sat.; 2:00 P.M.–10:00 P.M. (dinner only), Sun.

MANHATTAN BEACH   (718) 965-6589. Ocean Avenue (between Oriental Avenue and MacKenzie Street), Brooklyn. Lifeguard on duty 10:00 A.M.–6:00 P.M.

MEADOWLANDS   (212) 421-6600 (for New York Jets' office in New York City). East Rutherford, New Jersey. Sept.–Dec. Call for schedule and ticket prices.

METROPOLITAN MUSEUM OF ART   (212) 879-5500. East 82nd Street and Fifth Avenue, Manhattan. 9:30 A.M.–8:45 P.M., Tues.; 9:30 A.M.–5:15 P.M., Wed.–Sun. $5.00/adult; $2.50/student & senior citizen; free/under 12.

MUSEUM OF THE AMERICAN INDIAN   (212) 283-2420. Broadway and 155th Street, Manhattan. 10:00 A.M.–5:00 P.M., Tues.–Sat.; 1:00 P.M.–5:00 P.M., Sun. $2.00/adult; $1.00/student & senior citizen with I.D.; free/Native American.

MUSEUM OF BROADCASTING   (212) 752-7684. 1 East 53rd Street (near Fifth Avenue), Manhattan. Noon–5:00 P.M., Wed.–Sat.; noon–8:00 P.M., Tues. $3.00/adult; $2.00/over 13 student; $1.50/under 13 & senior citizen.

MUSEUM OF THE CITY OF NEW YORK (212) 534-1672. Fifth Avenue at 103rd Street. 10:00 A.M.–5:00 P.M., Tues.–Sat.; 1:00 P.M.–5:00 P.M., Sun. & holidays. Free.

MUSEUM OF HOLOGRAPHY (212) 925-0526. 11 Mercer Street (between Grand and Canal Streets), Manhattan. Noon–6:00 P.M., Tues.–Sun. $3.00/adult; $1.75/child & senior citizen.

MUSEUM OF MODERN ART (212) 956-7070. 11 West 53rd Street, Manhattan. 11:00 A.M.–6:00 P.M., Mon., Tues., Fri., & Sat.; 11:00 A.M.–9:00 P.M., Thurs.; noon–6:00 P.M., Sun. Closed Wed. & Christmas. $2.50/adult; $1.50/student; $.75/under 16 & senior citizen.

NASSAU VETERANS MEMORIAL COLISEUM Uniondale, Long Island.

NEW YORK AQUARIUM (718) 266-8500. Boardwalk West 8th Street, Brooklyn. 10:00 A.M.–6:00 P.M., daily (last admission 4:45 P.M.); 10:00 A.M.–7:00 P.M., weekends & holidays between Memorial Day and Labor Day (last admission 5:45 P.M.). $3.75/adult; $1.50/2–12 child.

NEW YORK BOTANICAL GARDEN (212) 220-8700. The Bronx. Grounds are open from dawn to dusk, daily; Conservatory open 10:00 A.M.–4:00 P.M., Tues.–Sun. $3.00 parking fee. Conservatory: $1.50/adult; $.75/under 12 & senior citizen (when show is not in progress); $2.50/adult; $1.25/child (when show is in progress); free/under 6.

NEW YORK CITY FIRE MUSEUM (212) 691-1303. 278 Spring Street (between Hudson and Varick Streets), Manhattan. Call for schedule and fee information.

NEW YORK CONVENTION & VISITORS BUREAU (212) 397-8222. 2 Columbus Circle, Manhattan. 9:00 A.M.–5:00 P.M., Mon.–Fri.; 10:00 A.M.–6:00 P.M., Sat., Sun., & holidays.

NEW YORK DOLL HOSPITAL (212) 838-7527. 787 Lexington Avenue (near 63rd Street), Manhattan. 10:00 A.M.–6:00 P.M., Mon.–Sat. Closed Sat. July–Aug.

THE NEW YORK EXPERIENCE (212) 869-0345. 1221 Avenue of the Americas (between 48th and 49th Streets), Manhattan. 11:00 A.M.–7:00 P.M., every hour on the hour, Mon.–Thurs.; 11:00 A.M.–8:00 P.M., every hour on the hour, Fri. & Sat.; noon–8:00 P.M., every hour on the hour, Sun. $4.75/adult; $3.75/senior citizen; $2.90/under 12.

NEW YORK PHILHARMONIC YOUNG PEOPLE'S CONCERTS (212) 580-8700. Avery Fisher Hall, Lincoln Center (West 65th Street and Broadway). Call for information. Tickets are mainly sold by subscription, but leftover seats are sometimes available.

NEW YORK STOCK EXCHANGE VISITORS CENTER (212) 623-5167/(212) 656-3000. 20 Broad Street (just south of Wall Street), Manhattan. 9:30 A.M.–4:00 P.M., Mon.–Fri. Free.

OMONIA CAFE (718) 274-6650. 32-20 Broadway (near 33rd Street), Astoria, Queens. 8:00 A.M.–3:00 or 4:00 A.M., daily.

ORCHARD BEACH (212) 885-1828. Pelham Bay Park, the Bronx. Lifeguard on duty 9:00 A.M.–6:00 P.M.

PAPER BAG PLAYERS (212) 362-0431. Call for schedule and location of shows.

PERFORMING ARTS REPERTORY THEATER (212) 595-7500. Call for schedule and location of shows.

THE _PETREL_ (212) 825-1976. Battery Park and South Ferry, Manhattan. Rates vary with length, day of week, and season; range from $6.00 to $17.00. Call for exact figures. Available for private charter.

PIONEER SAIL (212) 669-9400. South Street Seaport, Pier 16, Manhattan. Apr.–Oct., 3 sails a day on weekends. Call for schedule and rates.

PROSPECT PARK (718) 788-0055. Flatbush Avenue and Empire Boulevard, Brooklyn.

Carousel (718) 965-6522. Apr.–Oct. $.25/all.

Children's Farm (718) 965-6560. 10:00 A.M.–4:00 P.M., daily, Apr.–Sept. Free.

Zoo (718) 965-6560. 11:00 A.M.–5:00 P.M., daily.

PUPPET PLAYHOUSE (212) 879-3316. Murphy Center, 555 East 90th Street (by the East River), Manhattan. Call for information.

QUEENS BOTANICAL GARDEN (718) 886-3800. 43-50 Main Street, Flushing, Queens. 9:00 A.M.–sunset, daily. Free.

RADIO CITY MUSIC HALL   (212) 757-3100. 1260 Avenue of the Americas at 50th Street, Manhattan. Call for schedule and ticket prices.

RCA BUILDING   Rockefeller Center (behind skating rink). Between 48th and 50th Streets (between Fifth and Sixth Avenues), Manhattan.

RED CABOOSE   (212) 575-0155. 16 West 45th Street (between Fifth Avenue and Avenue of the Americas), Manhattan. 10:00 A.M.–7:00 P.M., Mon.–Sat.

RICHMONDTOWN RESTORATION   (718) 351-1611. Richmondtown, Staten Island. *Labor Day–June*: Noon–5:00 P.M., Sat. & Sun.; *July–Aug.*: 10:00 A.M.–5:00 P.M., Tues.–Sat.; noon–5:00 P.M., Sun. Grounds: Free. Buildings: $2.00/adult; $1.50/student; $1.00/6–8 child; free/under 6.

ROCKAWAY BEACH   (718) 634-7065. Beach Street to Beach 149 Street, Queens. Lifeguard on duty 10:00 A.M.–6:00 P.M.

ROCKEFELLER CENTER   (212) 489-4300 (for information about Christmas tree-lighting ceremony). The buildings between Fifth and Sixth Avenues and between 48th and 51st Streets, Manhattan.

   Ice-Skating Rink   (212) 757-6271. Oct.–May 1, 9:30 A.M.–10:30 P.M. (Closed 1:30–2:00 P.M. and 6:00–6:30 P.M.)

ROOSEVELT ISLAND TRAMWAY   East 60th Street and Second Avenue, Manhattan. One subway token each way; free/under 5.

ROUMELI RESTAURANT   (718) 278-7533. 33-04 Broadway (near 33rd Street), Astoria, Queens. 11:00 A.M.–1:00 A.M., daily.

RUMPLEMAYER'S   (212) 755-5800. 50 Central Park South (east of Avenue of the Americas and across the street from Central Park), Manhattan. 7:00 A.M.–1:00 A.M., daily.

ST. PATRICK'S CATHEDRAL   Fifth Avenue (between 50th and 51st Streets), Manhattan.

SERENDIPITY   (212) 838-3531. 225 East 60th Street (between Lexington and Third Avenues), Manhattan. 11:30 A.M.–midnight, Mon.–Thurs.; 11:30 A.M.–1:00 A.M., Fri., 11:30 A.M.–2:00 A.M., Sat.; noon–midnight, Sun.

SHEA STADIUM   (718) 507-TIXX. Flushing, Queens. Call for schedule and ticket information.

THE SILENT SKY   (212) 924-6381. 176 West Houston Street (at Avenue of the Americas), Manhattan. Noon–6:00 P.M., Mon.–Sun.

SKY RINK   (212) 695-6556. 450 West 33rd Street (near Tenth Avenue), Manhattan. Call for rates.

SKYSCRAPERS MENTIONED IN THIS BOOK   (all in Manhattan): *AT&T Building*, Madison Avenue and 55th Street; *Chrysler Building*, Lexington Avenue and 42nd Street; *Flatiron Building*, corners of 23rd Street, Fifth Avenue, and Broadway; *Grace Building*, 42nd Street between Fifth and Sixth Avenues; *IBM Building*, 57th Street and Madison Avenue; old *McGraw-Hill Building*, 42nd Street between Eighth and Ninth Avenues; *Metropolitan Life Building*, Madison Avenue and 23rd Street; *New York Life Building*, Lexington or Madison Avenues between 26th and 27th Streets; *Woolworth Building*, Broadway and Park Place. See separate entries for *Citicorp Center*, *Empire State Building*, and *World Trade Center*.

SOHO   Between Houston and Canal Streets (between Lafayette Street and the Hudson River), Manhattan.

SOUTH STREET SEAPORT   (212) 669-9400. Between Peck Slip and John Street (between Water Street and the East River), Manhattan.

SPANISH HARLEM   Between Park Avenue and the East River, above East 96th Street, Manhattan.

STATEN ISLAND CHILDREN'S MUSEUM   (718) 273-2060. 914 Richmond Terrace, Staten Island. *Sept.–June*: 2:00 P.M.–5:00 P.M., Wed.–Fri.; 11:00 A.M.–5:00 P.M., Sat. & Sun. *July & Aug.*: 1:00 P.M.–4:00 P.M., Tues.–Fri.; 11:00 A.M.–5:00 P.M., Sat. & Sun.

STATEN ISLAND FERRY   (212) 806-6940 (Manhattan)/ (718) 727-2508 (Staten Island). Battery Park and South Ferry, Manhattan; or Bay Street in St. George, Staten Island. Runs 24 hours a day, 7 days a week. $.25 from Manhattan to Staten Island; free from Staten Island to Manhattan.

STATEN ISLAND ZOO   (718) 442-3100. 614 Broadway, Staten Island. 10:00 A.M.–4:45 P.M., daily. Closed major holidays. Children's Zoo open May–Oct. $.75/adult; $.50/child; free/under 6 & senior citizen. Admission is free on Wed.

STATUE OF LIBERTY   (212) 269-5755. Liberty Island, Manhattan. Take the Statue of Liberty ferry from Battery Park. Call for schedule and rates.

SYMPHONY SPACE   (212) 864-5400. 2537 Broadway at 95th Street, Manhattan. Call for schedule of children's events.

TAVERN ON THE GREEN   (212) 873-3200. Central Park West and 67th Street, Manhattan. 1i:30 A.M.–3:30 P.M. (lunch), 5:30 P.M.–midnight (dinner), Mon.–Fri.; 10:00 A.M.–3:30 P.M. (brunch), 5:00 P.M.–midnight (dinner), Sat. & Sun. Reservations advised.

THIRD STREET MUSIC SCHOOL SETTLEMENT   (212) 777-3240. 235 East 11th Street (between Second and Third Avenues), Manhattan. Call for schedule of events.

TIMES SQUARE   Between Seventh and Eighth Avenues (between 41st and 53rd Streets), Manhattan.

TOWER RECORDS   (212) 505-1500. 692 Broadway (near 4th Street), Manhattan. 9:00 A.M.–midnight, daily.

TOY PARK   (212) 427-6611. 112 East 86th Street (between Park and Lexington Avenues), Manhattan. 10:00 A.M.–6:00 P.M., Mon.; 10:00 A.M.–7:00 P.M., Tues., Wed., Fri., & Sat.; 10:00 A.M.–8:00 P.M., Thurs.; noon–5:00 P.M., Sun. (Closed Sun. July–Aug.)

UNITED NATIONS BUILDING   (212) 754-7713 (for information)/(212) 963-4440 (for reservations). East 46th Street and First Avenue, Manhattan. 9:15 A.M.–4:45 P.M., daily. Hour-long tours begin approximately every half hour. $4.50/adult; $2.50/student & over 5 child. Children under 5 are not permitted.

VAN CORTLANDT PARK   (212) 549-6494. Broadway and West 242nd Street, the Bronx.

   Stables   (212) 543-4433. 8:00 A.M.–dusk, daily. Call for rates.

WALL STREET AREA   Everything south of the Brooklyn Bridge, Manhattan.

WORLD TRADE CENTER   (212) 466-7377 (observation deck). Between Liberty and Vesey Streets (between West and Church Streets), Manhattan. 9:30 A.M.–9:30 P.M., daily. $2.95/adult; $1.50/6–12 child; free/under 6.

YANKEE STADIUM   (212) 293-6000. The Bronx. Call for schedule and ticket information.

C·A·R G·A·M·E·S

Long car rides don't have to be boring or drive you crazy. Playing games will make the time fly by. You don't have to just sit still and get sore, stiff, and restless, either. Stretch out and move your tired muscles with some easy car exercises. They'll keep you from wishing you could roll down the window and scream, or kick open the door and jump out.

Games are for fun, so laugh it up and play the ride away.

Things to take along on any long ride:

- something hard and flat to write on, like a tray, board, or large hardcover book
- a roll of tape
- coloring pens, pencils, or crayons
- a pad of paper or notebook
- a deck of cards
- books to read

WORD GAMES:

Think of as many names as you can for each letter of the alphabet. *D*: Debbie, Doug, Diane, Denise, Dan, and so on.

Look for each letter of the alphabet on car license plates as they pass (skip the hard-to-find letters *Q* and *Z*).

Make words out of the letters you see on car license plates. Example: For 125 BHV, say *beehive*.

Packing for your trip: Name things you can put in your suitcase starting with the letter *A*, then *B*,

then *C*, and so on. For example: apple, baseball, cat, dictionary . . . (they don't really *have* to be things you need on your trip).

COUNTING GAMES:

Watch car license plates and count the numbers, starting with 0. See who can reach 9 first. Or, keep counting to 20—that takes longer.

Find the most: Pick something to count and see who can find the most. You can pick things like green cars, stop signs, license plates from California, people driving with hats on, kids in cars, and so on.

GUESSING GAMES:

20 Questions: Think of something that you want everyone else to guess. They ask you questions to try to figure out what it is. You can only answer yes or no. If they don't guess what you picked in 20 questions, you win. Or, you can just let them keep asking questions until someone figures it out.

Pictionary (like dictionary, but with pictures): Like *20 Questions*, someone is "it" and thinks of something that everyone else tries to guess. You draw pictures to give them clues and hints—but you can't draw what the answer is. You could pick the name of your school. Then, for clues, you would draw your classroom, desk, schoolbook, lunch box, or teacher, or anything else you might think of. Draw as many pictures as it takes for someone to guess what it is you're thinking of.

DRAWING:

One person draws a mark, line, shape, letter, or number, and someone else has to make a picture out of it.

STORIES:

One person starts to make up a story. The next person has to add the next line or sentence to the story, then on to the next person. Everyone in the car makes up the story line-by-line. It can turn out to be a pretty funny story; you might even end up on the moon with a _____.

Make up a travel friend: This is your chance to say anything you want about your trip. You pretend that you have an invisible friend taking the trip with you. Only you can see and hear your friend, so you have to tell everyone else what your friend is saying. Do they like your car? Where do they want to go tomorrow? What do they like to eat? You can say ANYTHING. Make up a story about where your friend is from, what his or her family is like, or whatever you want.

CARDS:

Bring along a deck of cards and play your favorite games or, if there's room, you can turn a hat over and try to toss the cards in it. You have to throw them like they're tiny Frisbees.

MOVEMENT GAMES:

Charades: Someone acts out a kind of animal (or anything else) just by using her or his face and hands. Everyone else has to guess what she or he is.

Simon Says: Someone is Simon, and everyone else has to do whatever Simon says—but only when Simon says "Simon says . . . ." If Simon doesn't say this and you do what he or she says, you goof. Like this: "Simon says touch your nose with your right hand." (Simon touches his nose. Everyone else does, too.) Simon gives lots of directions, then he sneaks in an order without saying "Simon says" but does it anyway. If anyone follows, they goof.

Statues: Everyone playing this game freezes into a statue. See who can stay that way without moving the longest.

Making Faces: Someone is "it." He or she makes a face—sad, goofy, happy, sleepy, cranky—and the other person has to imitate the face. This simple game is really a crack-up.

EXERCISES:

You'll be amazed at how much exercise you can get while riding in a car. You can't swim, run, or throw a ball, but you can work out by stretching your muscles. Make up your own stretches, or do the ones below. Remember to hold them to the count of 10 before you stretch another muscle. And don't forget to take a deep breath and blow it out slowly with every stretch. It's "car yoga."

Touch your toes. Stretch your arms straight out. Spin them in circles. Twist around as far as you can. Reach for the ceiling. Bend your head back. Bend it forward. Press your hands down on the seat next to you, and try to pick yourself up off the seat. Flex your feet up, then down, point your toes. Repeat this 10 times. You'll be surprised at how this feels on your stiff muscles.

Answers to Puzzles

page 11

J	I	B	G	X	O	F	R	O	I	L	M	T	C	S
Y	A	V	R	K	Q	X	N	E	A	Y	X	H	B	A
P	F	R	Z	O	C	H	U	D	S	O	N	E	Q	N
Q	Y	B	O	R	O	U	G	H	T	Q	P	B	U	T
S	E	K	O	D	A	K	D	B	A	Y	Z	R	Y	B
Q	U	E	E	N	S	U	L	C	T	F	P	O	V	D
T	W	E	R	B	E	D	L	Y	E	N	E	N	E	S
P	M	A	N	H	A	T	T	A	N	K	O	X	R	H
U	F	S	K	G	U	E	D	G	I	R	P	F	R	C
Z	A	T	L	A	N	T	I	C	S	M	L	J	A	O
G	B	R	O	N	C	K	S	H	L	S	E	W	Z	Z
J	T	I	N	V	L	A	G	Z	A	R	D	M	A	M
Z	I	V	O	H	G	M	X	I	N	Q	K	R	N	V
H	T	E	W	S	I	W	J	L	D	M	U	P	O	H
W	O	R	L	D	S	F	A	I	R	J	K	V	L	U

page 17

1. Warning/Slow down
2. Don't walk
3. Walk
4. Crosswalk
5. One-way street

page 20

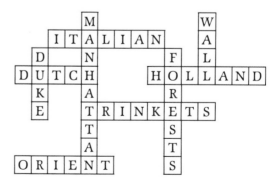

129

page 26

1. Empire State Building
2. St. Patrick's Cathedral
3. Chrysler Building
4. World Trade Center (Twin Towers)
5. Guggenheim Museum
6. United Nations

page 43

Upper West Side; Midtown; lower Manhattan (Wall Street area, financial district)

page 47

```
              F I F T H
                  I
        H A R L E M   N
      D         I       G A R M E N T
M I D T O W N   N       N
      A         C       C
      M         O       I
      O         L       A       F
      N         C E N T R A L P A R K   U
      D
```

page 65

```
G R I Z Z L Y   B E A R
M A S T O D O N
D I N O S A U R
A N T E L O P E
E L E P H A N T
K O M O D O   D R A G O N
```

page 51

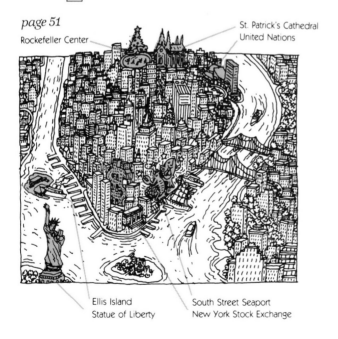

Rockefeller Center
St. Patrick's Cathedral
United Nations
Ellis Island
Statue of Liberty
South Street Seaport
New York Stock Exchange

page 73

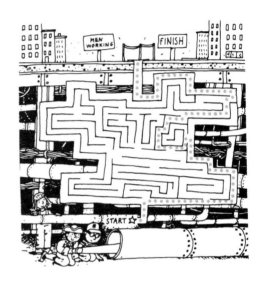

page 76

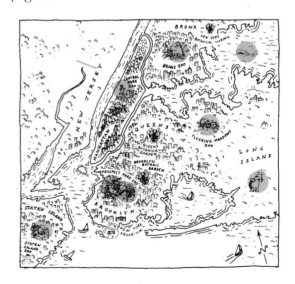

130

There are many different answers for this activity, but here is an example of what you could have answered.

A	**APE**	N	**NIGHTINGALE**
B	**BEAR**	O	**OSTRICH**
C	**CAT**	P	**PARROT**
D	**DOG**	Q	**QUEEN BEE**
E	**ELEPHANT**	R	**RHINOCEROS**
F	**FISH**	S	**SHARK**
G	**GOAT**	T	**TIGER**
H	**HORSE**	U	
I	**IGUANA**	V	**VAMPIRE BAT**
J	**JAGUAR**	W	**WALRUS**
K	**KOMODO DRAGON**	X	
L	**LLAMA**	Y	**YAK**
M	**MONKEY**	Z	**ZEBRA**

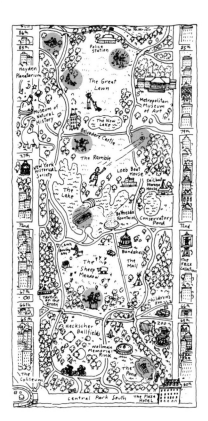

1. **CABBAGE**
2. **TOMATOES**
3. **POTATOES**
4. **CARROTS**
5. **SPINACH**

There are many different answers. Here are just a few:

baseball	dodgeball	lacrosse
basketball	football	soccer
billiards	jacks	softball
bowling	kickball	volleyball

1. tuba
2. violin
3. bass
4. French horn
5. clarinet
6. drum

PHOTO CREDITS
■ ■ ■ ■ ■ ■ ■ ■ ■ ■ ■ ■ ■ ■

I·N·D·E·X